BRIDGE BUILDING

*Creating connection and relationships between parents
and children/adolescents on the autism spectrum*

Kevin B. Hull

Bridge Building: Creating connection and relationships between parents and children/adolescents on the autism spectrum

by Dr. Kevin B. Hull

ISBN 13: 978-1-935986-44-7

Hullcounseling@tampabay.rr.com

www.Drkevinbhull.com

Lynchburg, VA
www.liberty.edu/libertyuniversitypress

This book is dedicated to the many parents and caregivers of children and adolescents diagnosed with Asperger's Syndrome and High Functioning Autism who shoulder a heavy load in loving and caring for their amazing young people. You inspire me endlessly and I admire your courage and dedication!

In Loving Memory of Dr. Ronald Allen,
a true Bridge Builder in every way.

Contents

Acknowledgements

I am truly grateful for all the wonderful professors, mentors, and colleagues that I have come in contact with over the years who have taught me so much and inspired me. I am also grateful for the many professionals who have labored endlessly in the pursuit of knowledge related to the causes and treatment of the disorders on the autism spectrum. Your work enables people like me to do what I do and without your research and writing many of us would be at a loss in helping these amazing young people.

To my amazing wife Wendy, your editing skill is truly remarkable and your love and encouragement provides me with endless energy to help others. To Dane, Jessica, Zane, Cade, Taylor and Katelyn I could never put into words how grateful I am for your love and support; I continue to renew my commitment to you daily to love, connect, and guide.

Finally, a special thanks to Hannah Coward for the interior and cover design, Brittany Meng for her editing expertise, and to Sarah Funderburke and the staff at Liberty Press for guidance, support, and encouragement.

CHAPTER 1

Worlds Apart: Parenting a Child Diagnosed with Asperger's and High Functioning Autism

Robin and Devin

Robin, a single mother of a twelve year old boy sits quietly as her son arranges his box of "special things" that he wants to show her. She wants to talk with him about a conversation that one of his teachers had with her regarding his lack of friends and how he has been alienating himself from others, and she waits patiently for an opening to begin the conversation. Devin, seemingly oblivious to her presence, murmurs to himself and works vigorously to carefully place all of his recent creations in a perfect line so that he can tell his mother all about them. Robin tries to relax and remain calm as she realizes that this is the same routine that she and Devin went through this morning before school, last evening, the day before and so on. She fights back tears as she secretly wonders why her son does not talk about girls, or sports, or show an interest in being with other children his same age.

"Ok, now here is what I wanted to show you!" Devin says excitedly. Devin begins sharing the same information about his creations that he shared that morning, the night before and every spare moment of every day before. Robin feels a sense of hopelessness and despair begin to creep over her. She knows if she interrupts him he will be angry and will shut down; yet if she sits without saying anything, his ramblings could go on for hours. She feels desperate to understand her son; yet unless they discuss a topic regarding one of his interests, he stares at her with a dull look waiting for her to finish and then bursts into a rant almost exactly at the same place she interrupted him. This is nothing new for Robin, but her worries have increased since he has become older. She thought Devin would grow out of it, hoping that his "issues" were simply an over-imaginative mind that would evaporate as he moved out of childhood.

Thinking back to Devin's younger childhood days, she remembered noticing that he acted differently than other children. By age four, Devin was "in his own little world" and showed odd patterns of speech as well as intense, focused energy towards things he liked. A movie that Devin enjoyed was not watched once or twice, but he craved it all day long for weeks. His favorite toy would be played with for hours upon hours; and if his routine was disrupted in any way, he would throw severe tantrums and nothing Robin tried would calm him down. When he began preschool, he had trouble adjusting to the routine and became overwhelmed by the number of children. More tantrums ensued; Teachers were frustrated and made calls to Robin at work. Robin tried another preschool. More tantrums; Robin was called, the teachers told her they have never seen "anything like this;" Robin then called the pediatrician who recommended medication and thought Devin must have "ADHD." She heard other diagnoses thrown around by other "professionals" such as Oppositional Defiant Disorder and Conduct Disorder. Robin vividly remembered feeling panic and a feeling of insanity coating her insides like black ink, oozing and spreading virus-like to every crevice of her being.

Robin remembered gathering her courage and strength to advocate for her precious son and throwing herself into "research mode." She searched relentlessly for answers on the internet. She was opposed to medication and firmly believed that somehow there must be other children like Devin; she constantly held hope that answers could be found. Robin observed him to be very sweet and loving in nature, especially when he and Robin functioned without deviation from their normal daily routine. She began to see that it was in situations that were new or contained circumstances out of Devin's control that he became combative. She battled constant thoughts since he was small that somehow she has done something wrong; *she* left his father who was abusive, *she* bumped his head on the side of the bathtub when he was three weeks old, *she* did not breast feed long enough. Each night Robin's sense of despair grew and she cycled through periods of being a fearless researcher and caretaker for Devin to feeling hopelessly sad and alone.

When she thought of Devin's gifts and talents, Robin was able to pull out of the state of despondency. He was very smart, with a sharp wit and wonderful "dry" sense of humor. He had a remarkable memory and was able to help her stay on track with her daily obligations. At age five or six he was beginning to branch out of some of his intense, repetitive interests. For instance, he had started to like cooking and was constantly looking for new recipes. He left the kitchen looking as if a grenade had exploded but Robin reminded herself that at least cooking was time spent together. He noticed the small things: the worm on the sidewalk, the bird egg under the bushes, the house number slightly leaning where it had not done so before. Some of his interests were fun to engage in, such as diving into the Harry Potter books and movies, which she herself came to love. When she stepped back and looked at things from another vantage point, her "favorite little guy" was like her in so many ways. She could be intense; she was smart; she wanted some things "just so," and she was forever being accused of being "stubborn" and "bull-headed" and so on. Robin also remembered not liking a lot of children when she was growing up. Her red hair and freckles made her feel as though she did not fit in and there was teasing that resulted in her learning to be content with being alone which she found not only delightful but much safer. Yes, she thought, she and Devin were more alike than Robin would like to admit at times. But she knew he was different from her and different from other children, from the way he intensely reacted to certain things to the way he poured himself into the activities and toys he loved. She sadly observed him being almost unable to join in group play with peers; instead, he stood on the sideline and watched the action, almost as if an invisible force prevented him from stepping into the swirl of action and finding his place within the group.

Diagnosis of Devin

Devin is typical of individuals who are diagnosed with Asperger's Syndrome (AS), a neurobiological developmental disorder found on the autism "spectrum[1]." Spectrum is a name given to include variations or different types of autism. AS, or High Functioning Autism (HFA) describes children who, like Devin, are of average int-elligence or higher but display unusual speech patterns and manner-isms, at times can appear awkward and clumsy, and who have difficulty with social interactions. Individuals diagnosed with AS/HFA sometimes display an obsessive, repetitive, and intense focus on a selected interest. For instance, a child may be interested in LEGO® Star Wars and talks or thinks about nothing else. An adolescent may live and breathe for a computer game and nothing else seems to matter.

---

[1] Attwood, T. 2007. *The Complete Guide to Asperger's Syndrome.* London: Jessica Kingsley Publishers.

An adult may be obsessed in reading a comic book that seems more appropriate for children. Individuals diagnosed with AS/HFA finds their specified interest to be the most important thing in the world. While many people have interests and "hobbies" the individual diagnosed with AS/HFA displays such intensity towards their interests that leaves literally no room for anything else. It is almost as if their brain works by focusing on one interest at a time, where neurotypical individuals (a term given for individuals not diagnosed with AS/HFA) typically tend to have several interests. I will discuss the clinical picture of AS/HFA in more detail in Chapter Two.

Struggles of Parents/Caregivers/Family Members of Individuals
Diagnosed with AS/HFA

The struggle of Robin trying to connect with Devin shows a common picture of fear, frustration, and guilt for parents or caregivers who are trying to parent their children diagnosed with AS/HFA. Parenting in general has not gotten any easier in these fast-paced, pressured times, but those parents or caregivers responsible for raising children and adolescents diagnosed with AS/HFA face additional struggles[2]. First, these children typically do not connect emotionally, socially, or physically in the same way as neurotypical children. The child may not make eye contact and may shy away from touching or hugging; and as the child grows older, he or she may continue to display a lack of interest in interacting and connecting with others, even family members. Most parents expect their child to desire closeness with them, and often feel slighted or rejected when their child does not naturally want to be cuddled. It is important to keep in mind that this does not mean that the child or individual does not desire closeness or connection; this is one of the most common misconceptions about individuals diagnosed with AS/HFA and one that this book seeks to correct. These differences that I have discussed are not a curse, but we must understand and remember that these individuals do not connect in the same manner physically, socially, or emotionally. Yet, despite these challenges, parents can find other ways of having meaningful connection with their child or adolescent diagnosed with AS/HFA.

---

[2] Attwood T. 1998. *Asperger's Syndrome: A Guide for Parents and Professionals.*
London: Jessica Kingsley Publishers.

A second struggle for parents or caregivers with children and adolescents diagnosed with AS/HFA is just the opposite of the above scenario. Instead of not desiring contact the child, adolescent, or adult is too connected with their primary caregiver (usually mom) and desires only that person and cannot tolerate being away from the parent or caregiver. This is called "separation-anxiety" and is fairly common in all children. However, for the child or adolescent diagnosed with AS/HFA, the separation-anxiety tends to be more intense, lasts much longer and can carry on through the adolescent years into adulthood. Some children and adolescents on the autism spectrum do not lash out angrily when they do not feel safe, but instead are very timid and go into "shut-down mode" desiring to be with the person whom they believe to be their only source of safety and security. Parents or caregivers with this type of child or adolescent diagnosed with AS/HFA often feel smothered and controlled by their child. I often hear tearful stories of feeling "trapped" and "tired," as well as the struggle that the parent or caregiver has lost a sense of personal identity. Many experience marriage problems and other relationship struggles as a result of the over-dependent child or adolescent. Chapters Four and Six contain specific information on strategies to break this cycle.

A third struggle for parents is battling negative feelings such as a sense of inadequacy, guilt, grief, and social embarrassment, among others. Many parents/caregivers of individuals diagnosed with AS/HFA experience a time of grief as they move through accepting that their child is different, as parenting their child requires a different set of parenting skills and a different mindset. Parents/caregivers of children and adolescents diagnosed with AS/HFA find themselves resisting society's constant pressure for a "normal" life and a "normal" child within a "normal" family, even though no one knows what "normal" means. I challenge parents to grieve the loss of "normal" as soon as possible, because until this happens they will not be ready to move into acceptance and see the positive aspects that AS/HFA brings, nor find the strength to weather the storms that often come with raising a child or adolescent diagnosed with AS/HFA. I often talk with parents who are afraid to take their child out in public for fear that the child will have a tantrum and embarrass them in some way. This fear must be worked through; many parents in this culture are conditioned to worry about what others think of them and feel as though they are performing on a universal stage for all to see and judge. Until the parent/caregiver of the individual diagnosed with AS/HFA learns to shed this concern, the parent will carry a heavy weight of self-consciousness and worry over what the lady in the checkout lane (whom she does not know) will think of her parenting skills while her child is throwing a royal fit over not being able to checkout in lane number six because he loves the number six.

This brings us to a fourth struggle for parents/caregivers of children and adolescents diagnosed with AS/HFA: The fear and knowledge that "My child does not fit in." Perhaps the greatest difficulty for parents/caregivers is when their precious child or adolescent or adult diagnosed with AS/HFA cannot find a place in the world. For the young child, the inability to connect with peers creates fertile ground for bullying and social rejection; the same is true for the adolescent. For the adult diagnosed with AS/HFA, there are the challenges of not only social connection but also of becoming independent, finding a mate, starting a career, and building a life. Parents and caregivers become frustrated as they try everything they can to get their child in activities and expose them to social situations. I encounter many parents or caregivers who believe that the child or adolescent will "get it" and become socially adept if given enough social exposure and practice. While research does show that it is helpful to give children and adolescents diagnosed with AS/HFA social exposure as a way to help teach better social skills, there is no "quick fix" to the social issues that individuals diagnosed with AS/HFA face[3]. There is also the risk of emotional damage by pushing the child or adolescent too hard which usually only results in frustration for both the young person and the parent or caregiver. I stress with parents that it takes a combined approach of patience, social skills training, and giving the child or adolescent every opportunity to practice social skills, despite how exhausting this can be for the parent/caregiver.

A fifth struggle that makes parenting a child or adolescent diagnosed with AS/HFA difficult is the communication deficits that many of these individuals share. The child or adolescent diagnosed with AS/HFA often struggles with understanding and communicating thoughts and feelings, even with people whom they feel safe. Conversely, the parent/caregiver may become frustrated with the child or adolescent because the child has difficulty comprehending what the parent is saying, not because the child or adolescent is not intelligent or does not possess the ability, but because of the way in which the information is received. Individuals diagnosed

---

[3] Rao, P. A., Beidel, D. C., and Murray, M. J. 2008. "Social Skills Interventions for Children with Asperger's Syndrome or High-Functioning Autism: A Review and Recommendations." *Journal of Autism and Developmental Disorders*, 38(2), 353–61. doi:10.1007/s10803-007-0402-4.

with AS/HFA tend to receive information differently than the way neurotypical individuals receive information. The case of Robin and Devin is a good example. Robin had information that she wanted and needed to share; however, had she attempted to do so before Devin was "ready" to receive it Robin would have felt like she was sharing the information with a tree (completely non-productive), or this attempt at sharing may have resulted in Devin becoming angry. She had learned to wait for an "opening;" but even then there was the possibility that Devin would not acknowledge that he heard the information or that what Devin had to say about the situation would not have helped Robin understand what Devin was thinking and feeling. Thus, many parents feel "shut out" of their child/adolescent's life; leaving the parent feeling resentful, hurt, and ultimately frightened.

A final struggle for parents/caregivers of children and adolescents diagnosed with AS/HFA that I will discuss here is the emotion of fear. I will explain later in Chapter Two how fear has an overall impact on the body and brain, disrupting the "executive functions" of the brain. The "executive functions" of the brain are related to memory, decision making (using logic and reasoning), and the ability to interpret one's emotions and the emotions of others. For parents or caregivers however, fear compounds the problem of connection, in that the parent's internal system interprets their child or adolescent's characteristics that are caused by AS/HFA as threatening, thus causing the parent or caregiver to subconsciously reject the child and build invisible walls to keep the young person at a "safe" distance. I teach the parent or caregiver in chapters Three and Five to learn to get rid of fear and to push through the inclination to distance themselves from their child where it feels "safe". I help the parent or caregiver see that their fear is a combination of the social pressure, the unknown (which always plagues us as humans), and a strong desire of thinking that the child or adolescent or adult is not going to be able to care for himself or herself and be independent. I strongly believe that for any parent or caregiver, getting rid of the fear response is necessary to both connect with our children as well as letting them go when it is time. Remember that fear and connection cannot exist together; you must learn to let go of the fear in order to fully build connection with your child or adolescent on the autism spectrum.

Robin and Devin Revisited

Robin's search finally paid off. She found a support group full of other moms and dads who had once felt helpless like she did. She found a child psychiatrist who specialized in working with children and adolescents on the autism spectrum who told her that she did not believe that Devin needed medications at this time. Robin also found a behavior analyst who helped her learn to manage Devin's outbursts and also gave her skills to structure the home to help them both function better together. For example, Robin was able to talk with Devin about the situation at school. She told him that she wanted to see what he needed to show her, but she also had something to share with him. Then she got a small timer and set it for 10 minutes. Devin knew that once the timer went off he had to take a "break" and listen to his mom. He understood that it would be her "turn;" he also knew that he was not in danger if he could not share everything that was on his mind. His counselor had helped him understand that other people want to share information too, and that was okay, even though he thought that what other people talked about was usually "boring."

The support group also led her to a counselor who conducted social skills groups and used play therapy to help Devin learn social skills as well as helped Robin better understand who he was and how he "ticked." Robin experienced a sense of peace and reassurance that while Devin's struggles as a result of AS/HFA brought challenges, there were also miracles that occurred daily because of him. She too had begun to notice the little things on their walks together that Devin showed her: the worm, the bird egg, the little details of houses, cars, and other objects. She realized that the "American Dream" and that "normal" was a myth and that these were cultural illusions that kept people from truly connecting with each other. She had come to relish and appreciate relationships in a new way as a result of working hard to connect with Devin.

The Purpose of this Book

This book was born out of my passion to help parents and caregivers of children, adolescents, and adults diagnosed with AS/HFA connect and form deeper relationships with these amazing individuals. I use a lot of stories as I always learn best when there is a picture painted to help me see something first before I tried to "do" it, and I have tried to do the same for you. I also want to help parents and caregivers learn to see the world through the eyes of their child, adolescent, or adult diagnosed with AS/HFA. I firmly believe that we must surrender our agenda and the viewpoints that our culture places upon us, so that the positive and miraculous aspects of these remarkable individuals are not missed. I do not ascribe to the "disease model" mindset that traditional psychology and medical science ascribes to. Yet, I realize that the medical world has something to offer. My therapeutic approach is based on what science can show us, but I adopt a strength-based, positive approach in my counseling work to help young people and families understand themselves and each other in order to build connections. I believe that relationships are vital in helping these amazing young people achieve their potential.

This is a hopeful era in which to be living for those parents and caregivers who have a child, adolescent, or adult diagnosed with AS/HFA and for those who work with these incredible individuals. There are many breakthroughs happening in the medical community, counseling field, and in the realm of education. Parents are becoming a powerful force and are being heard, and society in general has become more aware of the struggles as well as the gifts that these individuals truly represent through various books and films that represent AS/HFA in a positive way. I want to give you the gift of encouragement and hope most of all, and to help you, the parent and caregiver, to get rid of fear and discouragement so that you can fully connect with your child, adolescent, or adult. I am grateful to be able to share my work with you, and I am honored to help you and so many others on this journey of discovery.

CHAPTER 2

How AS/HFA is Diagnosed and Clinical Considerations
Diagnosis of Asperger's Syndrome and High Functioning Autism

I have set out to make this book as easy to read as possible. In my counseling work I like to keep things as simple as possible for the young people and adults with whom I work. I have found that the words I choose in my counseling sessions are powerful and I want to make sure that the people in my office have a clear understanding of themselves and their child. I have approached this book in the same manner, with the hope that you, the reader, will take away a good amount of knowledge and skills in helping your child. The best exercise that I ever had to do in my graduate training was to write a psychological report at a 5th grade level; the professor said that if a child can understand what it is you are trying to say, then you really have to know what you are talking about. I find that most people are very intelligent but have never received the necessary information in the right way that helps them understand the particulars of what life is like for a child or adolescent on the autism spectrum. That being said, I also believe that you should have an idea of what criteria is required for a diagnosis of AS and what doctors, psychiatrists, and psychologists are talking about when they say "clinical criteria", "diagnostic categories" and other big words. I also think that parents and caregivers should know the history of AS and how it came to be.

The story of AS begins with Hans Asperger, who was a child psychiatrist in Vienna, Austria. Asperger wrote a paper in 1944 in which he described a group of children he was working with that displayed difficulties in social interactions and expressing emotions. He noticed peculiarities in the children's communication style and awkward physical movements. Asperger's paper remained unknown until a woman named Lorna Wing coined the phrase "Asperger's Syndrome" in 1981 when she wrote about a different type of autism that eventually became known as "high functioning" autism. Asperger's paper was translated into English in 1991 by Uta Frith. This had an immediate impact on the medical and psychological community, and the creation of this category helped to separate higher functioning autistic children from children with more severe symptoms of autism that tend to be more shut-down emotionally and less verbal. Hans Asperger's writing was very detailed and contained empathy and compassion for the children that he described. Asperger did not blame the children's issues on the parenting style or the relationship that the child had with the mother. He recognized even then that heredity had something to do with the condition but also saw the gifts that the children possessed as well.[4]

Many parents often ask the questions, "Is diagnosis of my child important?" and "Should I get my child tested to determine if they have AS or not?" I answer these with a "yes and no" approach. On the "yes" side, diagnosis can be helpful because it can give teachers, school staff, and other professionals who come in contact with the child a picture of the child's challenges. At this time, there is a great deal of knowledge regarding AS/HFA and most professionals who work with young people are well aware of the characteristics. Diagnosis also provides a course for helping the young person with behavioral, social, and mental/emotional interventions, and having an official diagnosis can make the child and family eligible for certain services that would not be available without the formal diagnosis.

On the "no" side, the application of a label through diagnosis can reduce the individual to a name. For example, "There's Tommy, he's that Asperger's kid." This type of thinking dominates the culture where professionals in medicine, psychology, and education see the disorder or diagnostic label instead of the person behind the label. This is why I have purposely written this book in a style that implies that the child is separate from the label. For example, "A child *diagnosed* with AS/HFA" separates the child from the label and forces the reader to see them as a person first. Also, the diagnostic label can bring about a negative stigma about the young person, which can further alienate the child, particularly if the professionals who offer care are not educated about AS/HFA. I challenge parents or caregivers to get all the information prior to getting their child tested and reinforce the fact that whatever course they choose, their young person is and forever will be a real person with hopes, dreams, personality, and the chance to chart their own course in this world. I have never met two individuals diagnosed with AS/HFA who are exactly the same,

---

[4] Bromfield, R. 2010. *Doing Therapy with Children and Adolescents with Asperger Syndrome.* Hoboken, NJ: John Wiley & Sons Inc.

and like one mother said to me, "My child may have Asperger's, but Asperger's does not have him!"

Diagnostic Criteria

I briefly want to discuss the clinical criteria used to determine a diagnosis of AS/HFA. There are actual psychological tests that have been designed used in determining if a child meets the criteria for AS/HFA, and the clinical information that I am going to summarize is taken from the American Psychiatric Association Diagnostic and Statistical Manual (Fourth Edition, Revised) or the DSM-IV TR as it is commonly referred to in the mental health community[5]. I have purposely written this in easier to understand terms than what is found in the manual.

A.   The first category relates to problems with social interactions and requires two of the following four characteristics:

Problems using non-verbal behaviors like eye contact and gestures;

Failure to develop relationships with peers with people their own age;

Not sharing with other people interests, enjoyment, or achievements without being forced;

Lack of demonstrating a connecting feeling towards others in social situations

B.   The second category relates to the individual showing a lack of range in interests or behavior or activities and requires one of the following characteristics:

Being intensely preoccupied with an interest or interests that is out of the ordinary in intensity

Showing unchanging devotion to specific routines or rituals

Showing fixed and repeated motor movements (e.g., hand or finger flapping or twisting, or complex whole-body movements)

Being obsessed with parts of objects

C.   The characteristics cause problems in daily life functions (school, work, etc.)

D.   There is no language delay (began using words by age 2 and phrases by age 3)

E.   There is no delay in mental/intellectual development or being able to care for oneself (age appropriate) and is able to adapt and shows a curiosity about the world around them.

---

[5] American Psychiatric Association. 2000. *Diagnostic and Statistical Manual of Mental Disorders,* 4th ed., text revision. Washington, DC, American Psychiatric Association.

Gillberg's Criteria[6]

Many professionals prefer the criteria of Gillberg (1991) to identify AS because it includes the difficulties in speech and language that often accompany AS and because it is less harsh and easier to understand. I have chosen to include it here as well.

1. Severe impairment in reciprocal social interaction
  (at least two of the following)

       (a) Inability to interact with peers

       (b) Lack of desire to interact with peers

       (c) Lack of appreciation of social cues

       (d) Socially and emotionally inappropriate behavior

2. All-absorbing narrow interest
  (at least one of the following)

       (a) Exclusion of other activities

       (b) Repetitive adherence

       (c) More rote than meaning

3. Imposition of routines and interests
  (at least one of the following)

       (a) On self, in aspects of life

       (b) On others

4. Speech and language problems
  (at least three of the following)

       (a) Delayed development

       (b) Superficially perfect expressive language

       (c) Formal, pedantic language

       (d) Odd prosody (pitch, rhythm, tone), peculiar voice characteristics

       (e) Impairment of comprehension including misinterpretations of literal or implied meanings

---

[6] Gillberg, C. 1991."Clinical and Neurobiological Aspects of Asperger's Syndrome in Six Families Studied." In *Autism and Asperger's Syndrome* (ed. U. Frith), 122–46.

5. *Non-verbal communication problems*
    (at least one of the following)

    (a) Limited use of gestures

    (b) Clumsy/gauche body language

    (c) Limited facial expression

    (d) Inappropriate expression

    (e) Peculiar, stiff gaze

6. *Motor clumsiness:* poor performance on neurodevelopmental examination

As you can see, the clinical criteria encompasses all of the areas that are affected by AS/HFA, and this is the information used by professionals when attempting to diagnose a child, adolescent, or adult.

Additional Characteristics that Create Difficulties in Connecting

MINDBLINDNESS

In addition to the clinical criteria, there are other characteristics that create difficulty for the individual diagnosed with AS/HFA. The first characteristic is called mindblindness. Mindblindness is known as the inability of the individual to see a situation from another person's perspective and identify with another person's emotions[7]. Think of a tennis ball with a picture on one side of the ball. If I show you the picture on one side and turn the ball to the side that does not have the picture, your mind can still see the picture and you know that even though you cannot see the picture, it is still there. A person diagnosed with AS/HFA struggles with this when it comes to imagining the emotions of others or predicting the emotional responses of others. It is as if they cannot remember the picture on the other side of the tennis ball. This is why "Aspies" or "Aspergians" (as people diagnosed with AS/HFA are sometimes called) can appear uncaring and without empathy at times. Individuals diagnosed with AS/HFA struggle with mindblindness, particularly in childhood when developing a "theory of mind" (the ability to understand and predict the emo-

---

[7] Baron-Cohen, S. 1995. *Mindblindness: An essay on autism and theory of mind.* Cambridge, MA: The MIT Press.

tions of others) which is important in learning social skills. Thus, the individual has a hard time demonstrating empathy or putting himself or herself in another person's "shoes." These deficits in perspective taking cause difficulty for a number of reasons.

First, because the individual diagnosed with AS/HFA appears uncaring or "rude," peers tend to ostracize the person because people tend to interpret the lack of empathy as threatening. Second, mindblindness can make the individual diagnosed with AS/HFA as "boring," "dull," and lacking personality and charisma, which can lead to more social rejection. Third, mindblindness disrupts the building of relationships. Relationships are built on trust, and without empathy it is hard to create connection with others. A fourth reason that mindblindness causes problems is that individuals diagnosed with AS/HFA experience a great deal of rejection and often assume that people do not like them because of who they are, which further leads to isolating themselves from others and causes fear and dread when faced with social situations.

I want to reiterate that mindblindness represents a challenge for the individual diagnosed with AS/HFA, but it does not mean that these individuals cannot achieve closeness with another person or that the individual diagnosed with AS/HFA is doomed to walk the earth without social connection. It simply means that the person diagnosed with AS/HFA sees people and relationships in different ways. Individuals diagnosed with AS/HFA form deep, committed relationships and experience success in all walks of life. They get married and find joy in connecting with others. I remind parents/caregivers that each of us has our own personality style and we learn social skills at different "speeds;" there is no "normal" social learning style. I work with children and adolescents each day through social skills groups and individual counseling to help them understand social connection and develop a "theory of mind." While it may not occur naturally for them, I see each day how these remarkable young people are able to incorporate important social skills. We must remember that they *do* desire relationship and connection, but they do not always know *how* to do it.

Alexithymia

Alexithymia is known as the inability to understand, identify, and give meaning to emotions in oneself and others[8]. A high number of individuals diagnosed with AS/HFA display the trait of alexithymia and it creates challenges in many ways. First, alexithymia creates confusion for the individual diagnosed with AS/HFA which complicates the ability of the individual to form relationships with others. Managing one's emotions and being able to interpret the emotions of others is important in forming and sustaining relationships. For example, if a friend is angry it is important for me to recognize this because that emotional state is going to impact how much and in what way my friend is going to interact with me. Further, if my friend is angry with something I have done, it is important for me to know what happened so that I can find out what my friend is thinking and get to a resolution of the problem. The future of our friendship depends on this process. If, because of alexithymia, I did not learn to recognize the anger in my friend, or if I remained detached when my friend told me about something I did that hurt him, the friendship would have a major barrier that would need to be overcome for the friendship to continue. My friend may assume that I do not care about him or her, and choose to not want to be around me anymore. As you can see, alexithymia can severely hamper the creation of a relationship and disrupts necessary components that are needed for a relationship to go to a deeper level.

A second reason why alexithymia causes problems is in the area of emotional control. For the children or adolescents or adults diagnosed with AS/HFA, the complications caused by alexithymia can leave them feeling out of place and mentally disorganized, which often results in either shutting down/withdrawn behavior or lashing out. Neither of these behaviors is useful in building or sustaining relationships and leads to further social rejection and isolation. The person becomes fearful of emotions, and many tend to stay in the shut-down state in order to self-protect and go to great lengths to avoid social contact. I have had adolescents tell me that it is "easier" to avoid people and social settings so "I won't get hurt." Children and adolescents may also demonstrate "tantruming" behavior although parents/caregivers will find no apparent trigger for the outburst. I find that a great deal of my work with adolescents and young adults is to help them overcome this fear of emotion that is left over from years of rejection and misunderstanding the emotions of others. A major part of individual therapy consists of helping the young people or adults understand their own emotions and the emotions of others so that they do not go into "fight-or-flight" mode.

---

[8] Fitzgerald, M. and Bellgrove, M. A. (2006). "The Overlap between Alexithymia and Asperger's Syndrome." *Journal of Autism and Developmental Disorders,* 36(4), 573–576. doi:10.1007/s10803–006–0096–z.

Stress and "Fight-or-Flight"

One of the common complaints that I hear made by parents of children and adolescents is in regards to the explosive behavior that sometimes accompanies AS/HFA. What I try to get parents/caregivers to see is that for these individuals, there are many "triggers" that are severely irritating and that constantly drain the energy that is used to cope with daily life. For instance, a small child that was diagnosed with AS came to my office and her parents explained that she was experiencing sensory overload and would begin to tantrum if forced to wear a certain type of clothing. Her brain worked overtime to notice the slightest irritation that for most people would easily be ignored, but for her brain and skin, certain materials felt like barbed wire. This caused this little girl to be in constant pain and she would go into a "fight-or-flight" state resulting in crying, screaming, and eventually tearing off her clothing to be "free" of the constricting clothes. Neurotypical individuals typically do not have the severity of the "triggers" that individuals diagnosed with AS/HFA tend to have. I tell parents that if you can imagine something that literally drives you crazy, multiple that many times over and you have a picture of what life can be like for these individuals.

The "fight-or-flight" process that is described above is a result of the sympathetic nervous system that becomes triggered when our brains determine that we are in danger because of a threat in our environment. This threat can be real or imagined. Once the threat is identified, a chain reaction happens in the body that includes an increase in heart rate and breathing, shut-off of appetite and immune system, a change in the muscles, and a release of chemicals in the brain to name a few. The body prepares itself to either run away from the threat or to fight the threat in order to survive. Another occurrence that happens in the arousal of the sympathetic nervous system occurs in the frontal lobes of the brain. The frontal lobes are important because this is where decision making, logic/reasoning, and control of emotions are contained. When a person is in "fight-or-flight," the frontal lobes "disengage" and logic and reasoning go out the window because there is little time to analyze a situation when our life is threatened.

However, there are very few times when our lives are actually threatened in our culture, but the stress many people live under in modern day America puts strain on our internal systems that simply go into action when our brain tells the rest of our body that there is danger. Even if the "danger" is being late to a meeting or missing a deadline, the internal systems interpret this as life-threatening. The brain of an individual diagnosed with AS/HFA tends to work "overtime", scanning the environment for danger. This is why many of these individuals have rituals and routines because those serve to provide a sense of safety and control. This is important for parents/caregivers to understand because when a child or adolescent diagnosed with AS/HFA is "triggered" this process is taking place. It is not that the young person is spoiled, bad, or purposely trying to hurt anyone; the brain has interpreted a situation or person as a threat and their brain is in the "fight-or-flight" state. It is very hard for a parents and caregivers to not be reactive emotionally when they see this process going on in their child. However, I remind parents and caregivers that yelling, hitting, or fighting with their child is only going to make things worse. I teach parents and caregivers strategies to stay out of "fight-or-flight" and keep their logic and reasoning in place when dealing with emotional and physical outbursts of their child/adolescent diagnosed with AS/HFA.

"Fight-or-flight" is a factor that comes into play when considering alexithymia. Because the frontal lobes are important in a person's ability to manage emotions, and because individuals diagnosed with AS/HFA often have trouble with understanding personal emotions and the emotions of others, alexithymia can easily trigger the individual into a state of "fight-or-flight," which then leads to the shutting down behavior or lashing out that I discussed earlier[9]. It is difficult, if not impossible, to learn something when in the "fight-or-flight" state, and this may be why children diagnosed with AS/HFA have such a hard time recognizing social cues and learning social skills. I work with many individuals diagnosed with AS/HFA in my office that have experienced cycles of "fight-or-flight" so many times from negative social experiences that their brains are "stuck" in this state. Gradually, they can be taught to reinterpret social situations as non-threatening. By learning to keep the "fight-or-flight" process from being triggered, the individual diagnosed with AS/HFA can learn to overcome the fears and experience new situations and relationships.

What Does All this Mean?

I have given you a lot of information in this chapter with the purpose of helping you understand how the "professional" world sees AS/HFA. The main thing for

---

[9] Attwood, Tony. 2006. "Asperger's syndrome and problems related to stress."
In *Stress and coping in autism*, 351-370. New York, NY US: Oxford University Press, 2006.

you to remember is that it is hard for these individuals to see things from another's perspective, and they have difficulty in understanding their emotions and the emotional reactions of others. "Fight-or-flight" disrupts a parent/caregiver's ability to connect with his or her child or adolescent and this process seems to be triggered very easily in children and adolescents diagnosed with AS/HFA. The following chapters will help lay a foundation for connection and relationship as I will share specific techniques for you to build a stronger relationship with your child or adolescent diagnosed with AS/HFA.

CHAPTER 3

Relationship Barriers and Parent Qualities Necessary in Building Connection
with Children Diagnosed with AS/HFA

We have looked at the clinical "stuff" and now I want to look at "why" it can be hard to connect with your child diagnosed with AS/HFA. There are many characteristics of children diagnosed with AS/HFA that make it hard for parents to bond with them, and I often have to help parents understand those characteristics before the parents can build deeper connection with their child. We will also examine some qualities that are necessary for parents/caregivers to understand and acquire for the bonding process to occur.

Relationship Barriers

Children diagnosed with AS/HFA tend to have problems building connection with other people. Sometimes the child acts as though other people do not even exist; adults can often feel rejected, disrespected, or shunned. Many of the parents that I work with feel like they have done something wrong when their child does not attach to them and I work hard to help them see that there are characteristics of AS/HFA that make connection difficult. I want to give parents and caregivers encouragement and cheer them on so they will keep trying to connect and build relationship with their child. Thankfully, there is hope for building a strong and meaningful connection with your child diagnosed with AS/HFA! The barriers I will discuss here are things that can be improved and some are a "phase" that many children diagnosed with AS/HFA move through on their journey of development.

In Their "Own Little World"

One common characteristic of AS/HFA is when a child appears to be in his or her "own little world." Parents and caregivers often see a blank stare or observe that the children diagnosed with AS/HFA are completely oblivious to what is going on around them. Parents/caregivers often feel very frustrated or disrespected when this happens and take it personally, assuming that the child is ignoring them purposefully. I often hear parents say things like: "My kid hates me;" "They won't listen to me;" "I think my child is never going to talk to me again;" "We don't have anything in common." The root of the parent's feelings is fear and I challenge the parents to get rid of the fear in order to better understand their child by teaching them about the characteristics of AS/HFA. I help the parent experience a "perspective shift" to see things from a different vantage point. The child is not rejecting them; the child in fact loves them and feels safe enough with the parent to drift into their own little world; the child's brain simply does not allow these children to express themselves in the way that the parent expects them to. This shift is very important because once the parents shift their perspective, they are able to pull out of negative and "scarcity" thinking (a term I will explain this later in this chapter) and move to positive, "abundance" type thinking.

Communication Difficulties

Communication difficulties also contribute to relationship barriers between children and caregivers. One of the hallmark characteristics of AS/HFA is the difficulty that the individual has in both giving and receiving information. Parents often feel like they are "talking to a tree" and feel a great deal of frustration when they get a blank stare from their child after simple requests such as "put their shoes away" or when the parent tries to find out why the child is upset. Most parents expect their child is going to be able to tell the parent what is wrong when the child is visibly upset; however, children diagnosed with AS/HFA have difficulty doing so. Part of the difficulty is that these children tend to be "disconnected" from what is going on inside them and find it impossible to put feelings into words so that others can understand. I explained earlier how "fight-or-flight" can disrupt the ability to communicate effectively even in neurotypical individuals, so it is no wonder that these children display communication difficulties when upset. Most parents want to find out the reason a child is upset; our thinking is if we find the reason we can either 1) avoid the situation next time; or 2) give the child guidance so they learn to control themselves. However, when the child simple goes into "shut-down" mode, it can be a frightening experience for a parent and leave the caregiver feeling helpless and alone.

Behavioral Problems

Many children diagnosed with AS/HFA exhibit problematic behaviors which disrupt the bonding and relationship process between parents and child. Because these children tend to have many "high maintenance" characteristics that I discussed earlier, they tend to act out and lose control very easily when things do not go the way these children expect. Parents and caregivers usually tell me stories of having problems from the time the child was born, describing the child as "colicky" and then experiencing intense tantrums around the time the child began walking. Complicated by the communication difficulties that I discussed above, the child is usually unable to give the parent a clear reason for the behavioral acting out, which further frustrates the parent. These behavioral problems also make the parent feel as though they are in "prison," being afraid to take the child out in public places as well as being fearful of putting others in charge of their child while the parent seeks a much needed break.

One of the main problems I find that occurs as a result of the behavioral problems is that parents see themselves as worthless and incompetent and begin to view the child as a "threat." Parents often tell me of living on "eggshells," terrified that making one false move will push their child over the edge, resulting in a royal tantrum that may last several hours. Even when the child behaves appropriately, the parent is not sure what the combination was to make the desired behavior occur and there are usually a number of routines with so many steps that the parent feels overwhelmed and frustrated because it is impossible to follow the routine every day. Often, what the parent deems as safe and appropriate is different from what the child wants, and it is a classic power struggle. I challenge parents to take control of these types of situations because, the truth, is the child wants to know where the boundaries and limits are even though he or she may buck against them.

Parents should keep in mind never to take the behavior of the child diagnosed with AS/HFA personally: The child is not purposely doing this to you! Also, the child is not "Bad" or "Oppositional-Defiant." However, please know I am not completely excusing inappropriate behavior either. You will see in the final chapter of this book that I do believe that as parents and caregivers, we are responsible to show our children where the boundaries are and to provide consequences that teach our children appropriate behavior. I explain to parents of children diagnosed with AS/HFA to keep in mind that for these children who do act out, it is their brains and bodies zooming into "fight-or-flight" because there is a thought running through their brain of *"if I don't get what I want I will die!"* I tell parents to imagine the most miserable, intolerable situation they can imagine and then multiply that times 1,000, complete with the emotional and physical reactions, and this is what is like for a child diagnosed with AS/HFA who does not get a favorite food or has to change a routine unexpectedly. To a neurotypical individual, it is simply eating pork chops instead of macaroni-and-cheese because someone ate the rest of the macaroni-and-cheese; to the child diagnosed with AS/HFA it is a matter of literal "life-or-death." Once we understand this, the behavioral issues begin to make sense, and by maintaining a sense of control and being non-reactive, the parent can deal with the behavior much more effectively.

Emotional Problems

Children diagnosed with AS/HFA usually have trouble controlling their emotions and understanding the emotions of others[10]. To these children, emotions are strange sensations that cannot be controlled, and these strange sensations arise when these children do not get what they want. I find that negative emotions such as anger, fear, sadness, and frustration, (just to name a few) can act like gasoline on a fire that immediately triggers the "fight-or-flight" system resulting in the child crying, yelling, screaming, hitting, kicking, or throwing things. Once this cycle occurs, it is very easy for it to continue: The negative emotions trigger the behavior and so on. The main thought running in the background is *"something is not just right and I am going to die!"* For instance, one boy that I worked with would begin knocking things over and throwing things in his tantrum cycle. What was interesting is that this boy did not like loud noises, yet when he became upset he would scream (which further put him in a state of "fight-or-flight") and then break things which caused more noise which continued a new cycle of tantrum behavior. The goal for the therapist and the parent(s) is to teach the child to tolerate negative emotions and learn to understand them, but this is no easy task with children diagnosed with AS/HFA.

---

[10] Gellar, L. 2005. "Emotional Regulation and Autism Spectrum Disorders." *Autism Spectrum Quarterly.* (Summer, 2005). Retrieved from www.aspfi.org/documents/gellerasq.pdf.

To deal with negative emotions, the children diagnosed with AS/HFA often follow "rituals" that they think will keep the "bad" emotions away. Eating the same food, hand washing, only wearing certain types of clothing or shoes, and chanting certain words are just a few examples of this. I meet children who have to turn around three times before going through a doorway, some have to check the legs of a couch or chair before sitting in it, and I have seen some who only eat the same food every day three times a day. Both the behavioral and emotional problems of children diagnosed with AS/HFA are often rooted in "rituals" that the child follows in order to ward off negative emotions. This is actually practical, survival behavior. As humans we will do whatever we think is necessary to avoid being in an uncomfortable physical or emotional state: Human beings just do not like to be uncomfortable because deep down there is a sense that *"I am not safe."* Because of this pattern of behavior, many children diagnosed with AS/HFA are labeled as "OCD" (Obsessive-Compulsive Disorder) which is simply a term to describe a cycle of thinking and behavior that is done in a repeated manner in order to make the individual feel safe. Hopefully, this explanation will help you understand your child or adolescent's emotional and behavioral reactions and give you a different perspective in the way that you view your child or adolescent's rituals and routines.

Emotional problems are a huge factor in disrupting relationship building. Much like behavioral problems mentioned above, the parent is triggered emotionally when they see the warning signs of their child losing control, and the root of it all is fear. Fear that I, as the parent, will not be able to control my child, fear that I may get hurt, fear of social embarrassment, fear that my child will never, ever be "normal," and that my child will die without me to care for him for the rest of his life. So parents either resort to trying to control every step their child makes or they simply begin to reject the child. This rejection is usually not an outright rejection; but instead is a gradual building of an emotional wall that the parent hides behind, being cautious not to get too close, being content to leave the child in his or her "little world." The parent morphs into a "robot caregiver," only providing the base needs of the child but foregoing any relationship-building interaction because the parent believes her or she may be emotionally wounded or rejected.

Family life with children diagnosed with AS/HFA can be a roller coaster to say the least. The emotional problems of children and adolescents diagnosed with AS/HFA can disrupt marriages (usually there is a disagreement on how to handle the tantrum behavior) as well as the relationship between the children and adolescents diagnosed with AS/HFA and their siblings. This is also why the child diagnosed with AS/HFA is often rejected socially. Neurotypical peers, siblings, and adults often see the child as:

1. *Weird* (I do not understand them)

2. *Inflexible* (The child diagnosed with AS/HFA always has to be in control and because of the need to minimize anxiety, we have to follow the child's rituals)

3. *Too Much Work* (The amount of energy needed to interact with the child diagnosed with AS/HFA is exhausting and I can find something else to do)

4. *Unpredictable* (I never know when Tommy is going to explode and hurt me or start throwing things, screaming, etc.)

I encountered one family who explained that the family dog had begun to shake in fear when the child diagnosed with AS/HFA came into the room because of the unpredictable behavior of the child. When I work with families, much of my work is helping the parent and siblings to understand the thinking and feeling cycles of the child diagnosed with AS/HFA in order to help build better connection. I will discuss this later in chapter Four and Six when I share techniques that can be helpful in doing this.

Parent Skills Necessary in Building Relationship with Children Diagnosed with AS/HFA

The following section explains the characteristics that parents need to adopt to begin building relationship with their child diagnosed with AS/HFA. Because children diagnosed with AS/HFA have unique needs, parents need to be unique in creating a pathway to relationship. I want to give a word of encouragement here: This requires a new shift in perspective and thinking, which takes time. Do not get discouraged! This will be slow-going with some setbacks from time to time, and will seem like an uphill climb in the beginning. Parenting in general requires a shift in thinking and behavior as our children grow through new developmental stages, so, the truth is, we have to be ready to change and grow much like our children grow.

BE NON-REACTIVE

I have talked a great deal already about "fight-or-flight" and I mentioned in an earlier section of this chapter how parents/caregivers become triggered and go into an emotional state when the child loses control. This is natural because a parent's greatest job is to keep the child safe from harm. When a child is displaying tantrum behavior the parent's first thought usually relates to harm (*"my child is hurt!"*) which ramps up the "fight-or-flight" system immediately and puts the parent in "fear mode." Once the parent realizes that the child is not hurt, there is a natural instinct to soothe the child and get the child to stop (which usually does not work) and then the parent enters "frustration/fear mode" and usually thinks thoughts such as *"there is something wrong with them"* or *"there is something wrong with me as a parent otherwise my child would stop"* because the parent is attempting to apply logic to a completely emotional, fear-based situation. Once the parent realizes the child is not going to stop, and there is nothing the parent can do to calm the child down ("failure") the emotion of anger now joins frustration/fear and this is when the parents begin to yell, or may get physical (*"if I shake them or spank that will work!"*) having their own tantrum right along with the child. It is no wonder that we as parents attempt to seek shelter from these thoughts and feelings when they surface. The parent/caregiver yearns for peace, and when there is peace (*"if there is peace then my child is okay and I am safe"*) the parent or caregiver does not want to do anything to disrupt the peace, which leads to the child to following his or her rituals ultimately resorting in everyone in the home giving the child diagnosed with AS/HFA complete control.

Please understand that I am not trying to paint a picture that all children diagnosed with AS/HFA are out of control and exhibit wild behaviors and are impossible to live with. I love these children and adolescents, but many of the young people I come across who are diagnosed with AS/HFA lose control when they cannot be in control and I am trying to give parents/caregivers tools and understanding when they find themselves in those situations. I am passionate about the fact that it is impossible to build relationship when fear/frustration/anger are churning and the parent views the young person as a "time bomb" that may go off at any second. Many parents/caregivers who come to see me say, *"Ok, great, you have nailed it right on the head. This is what happens in our house, but how in the world am I supposed to be non-reactive when all this is going on?"*

A colleague of mine named Frank Schultz shares an exercise in his book *A Language of the Heart*[11] that details how one can turn off the "fight-or-flight" system. The exercise involves relaxing the core muscles of the lower stomach. I tell people to take a deep breath and then release the air slowly. As the air goes out, I encourage them to simply let their stomach muscles "unclench," letting the belly go soft. By keeping the belly soft, one will notice a shift in the muscles of the body and will begin to feel "blob-like." I usually observe people's shoulders immediately go down and they tell me they feel heavier. There is a reason for this. By releasing the stomach muscles, all the tension in the body is released. Once this happens, the "fight-or-flight" system turns off because the brain and body sense that there is no danger and no need to get ready to run or fight. Another interesting thing that happens is the frontal lobes of the brain (where our logic/reasoning and decision-making ability come from) came back "online." This part of the brain shuts off when we become emotionally aroused and enter "fight-or-flight" and is why people look back on an emotional experience and often state in misbelief "I can't believe I did that" or "I can't believe I said that". This phenomenon is what children and adolescents experience that are in "tantrum-mode," which is why I tell parents never to argue or try to reason with an angry child.

This exercise is useful because it grounds us to the moment. We only exist in this present moment. We cannot go forward or backward one second. The past is gone; it does not exist in the present moment. Yes, as humans, we bring our memories of the experience of the past (with emotions, thoughts, and patterns of reacting) with us to this present moment. However, when my body is not tense and my frontal lobes are engaged, I am not interpreting anything in my environment as threatening. Even if I am in the presence of a child throwing a tantrum, I know that I do not like it, but I am not in danger. Once I have determined that the child is not in danger and is simply upset because of not getting what is wanted, I can remember that I have choices. I can speak calmly. I can remove myself from the situation and step away. I can give off a presence that is calm, firm, and in control. This is powerful because it can help de-escalate the child and help them find his or her center as well.

---

[9] Schultz, D. Franklin. *A Language Of The Heart, Therapy Stories That Heal.* 2005.

This is powerful for building relationship because you as the parent are modeling a sense of peace, calmness, and being in control. Please know that by "non-reactive" I do not mean passive by any means. In fact, by being non-reactive, we as parents can be more active and prepared to intervene because we are thinking clearly, instead of being on guard in a "fight-or-flight" state. We are able to send the message to the child that while we are not happy with their behavioral choice, we still love them and have not rejected them. We are also in a calm, controlled state of mind that allows us to direct other children if they are present, think of appropriate consequences (more on that later in Chapter Seven!) and save our energy for other things. Being non-reactive is one of the most important elements in building relationship with children diagnosed with AS/HFA.

GET A THICK SKIN; DON'T TAKE IT PERSONALLY!

A second important characteristic for parents/caregivers of young people diagnosed with AS/HFA is to develop a thick skin. Because of the social difficulties that young people diagnosed with AS/HFA have in building relationship, parents/caregivers often feel rejected and ignored. This triggers many emotions and thoughts, and I find that many parents begin to believe that the child does not love them, which is not true at all. This is why I have included the poem in the back of the book written by John Greally, who wrote a letter to his parents as an adult remembering how he felt as a child when his parents perceived that he did not love them because he did not like hugs or return affection in the way they expected. I think this poem serves a wonderful reminder to the parents of these remarkable young people that not only are the parents and caregivers loved and appreciated, but that the child or adolescent does think about the parent or caregiver. It just comes in a different package.

In order to develop a thicker skin, the parent or caregiver must shift their thinking and expectations. The parent must shift their thinking towards this thought: *"I will show my child I love them by protecting them, providing for them, spending time with them and setting limits."* The parent/caregiver must get rid of any thought of getting anything in return. This thought is purposeful and intentional, and it removes the measuring scale mentality that "I will only love someone if I get the right amount of love back and it must be in the form that I desire." This new thought gets rid of the conditionality idea of love as well, which is so detrimental to building relationships. When I work with children in my office, I work to let them know that there is nothing they could do that would make me reject them. I set boundaries and show them limits, but I let the young person know that I do not see them as "bad" or "broken." My office must be a safe place first, and then the therapeutic relationship which is involves demonstrating unconditional acceptance of the child can be built. Any parent/caregiver wanting to build relationship with the child diagnosed with AS/HFA must send this message. However, the reality is, it is very, very hard to continue to give love to someone and get nothing back. Yet, this is where the shift in thinking is so important.

The second part of the shift for parents involves recognizing how their child diagnosed with AS/HFA shows love. I mentioned earlier how I have never met two individuals diagnosed with AS/HFA who are exactly the same, and the same is true when it comes to displaying and receiving affection. One of the most common myths about individuals diagnosed with AS/HFA is that they are cold, uncaring robots who insult everyone they meet. Not true! In fact, individuals diagnosed with AS/HFA are some of the most loving and affectionate people I have ever come in contact with! However, each child, adolescent, and adult shows affection in different ways. I challenge parents/caregivers to fully understand their child and throw out any expectations and any idea of what "normal" is and to fully grasp their child's way of showing love. I help parents understand that when a child diagnosed with AS/HFA is sitting quietly playing or "in their own little world" that this is an expression of "Hey, Mom, Dad, I feel good and I feel safe and I am really glad to be alive and thanks for making the world a safe place for me." I have been able to see many different forms of affection from children and adolescents over the years, from leaving little notes and messages scribbled on white boards and sticky notes, to hugs, high fives, and smiles. The point is that as you get to know your child, you will learn how they choose to show love and affection, and your only goal is to simply accept those forms of love and affection and send the message back to your child or adolescent.

Patience

One of the greatest qualities for any parent to develop is patience. Patience is a foundational component of relationship building because it is the foundation for understanding, controlling emotions, and modeling unconditional acceptance and love. It is also one of the essential elements in being able to teach, and I remind parents all the time that they are the greatest teacher their child will ever have. Much of how children learn is from watching the parent/caregiver in certain situations. Children are keen observers and in my experience, children diagnosed with AS/HFA are some of the best as they seem to miss nothing. When the parent/caregiver models patience, the child incorporates this quality into his or her bundle of attributes. Also, the child's sense of safety remains intact, because the parent's reaction plays a large role in whether the child will spin into "fight-or-flight" mode.

A SENSE OF HUMOR

I use humor in my counseling sessions whenever appropriate because it can help remind us that even in the midst of crisis there are funny things. Ellen DeGeneres found comedy as a result of being in the worst pain of her life following the death of a friend, and her first comedy routine involved an imaginary phone call to God to search for answers. She performed it on Johnny Carson's Tonight Show and was the first woman comedienne on the show to be called over to "the couch" after a routine. What a wonderful picture of dealing with a tragedy! I have worked in very difficult environments with challenging situations with desperate and hurting people, and if I (and my colleagues) did not find a way to laugh and have fun, we would not be very effective. We must find a way to interject humor into our struggles because it helps us not take things too seriously and helps ward off the dread of the unknown and the "what-ifs."

The difficult part for parents/caregivers is that parenting and caring for a child diagnosed with AS/HFA can be an exhausting task and many are not "in the mood" to laugh at anything. This is what "survival mode" does to us; every situations is interpreted as very dire and there is no energy left over for laughter. What I tell parents/caregivers to do is to adopt an observatory role which helps to pull out of being "in" the situation to simply "watching" a situation. Many of us have laughed at a movie or TV show that shows a situation in which everything is all wrong, yet if we were in the situation or knew people personally in the situation we might actually cry. The TV scenario is funny because it is something we are watching, not something we must fix or change. I remind parents that we cannot, or need to "fix" the children diagnosed with AS/HFA. They do not need fixing; they need loving and guiding and opportunities provided to them for the possibility of growth. By being non-reactive, getting rid of fear, and adopting an observing stance, we are more able to see the humorous side of things.

Be Fearless!

I often ask people in my counseling office "What is the worst thing that can happen?" when they are sharing their fears with me. The question forces them to imagine the most terrible thing and put words to the feeling of fear. I help people see that the thing we fear the most is the unknown and human beings spend a great deal of time "what-if-ing." I help ground them to the moment and see that we exist in this moment of time, yet our brains want to help us stay safe and so it imagines the worst thing that could possibly happen so that if it happened we would somehow be prepared for it. However, this is very destructive and damaging to building relationship. This fear rips parents from the moment and propels them into the future where we neither exist nor can do anything about the things that are imagined. Parents of children diagnosed with AS/HFA have a great deal of fears about the future. They tell me they imagine their child homeless, beaten up, or killed and can rarely imagine the child growing up and being a successful adult because of the behavioral, emotional, and relationship issues that we have discussed earlier.

However, in order to build relationship with children diagnosed with AS/HFA the parent or caregiver must get rid of fear. They must shed the fear of the future, the fear of not being "enough," and the fear that their child is doomed. This is why I am so passionate about people "staying in the moment" and learning to turn off the "fight-or-flight" process because people cannot be in the moment and build relationships when the fear of the future is pressing in on them. Parents do need to be aware of their children's needs in order to provide for them in a proper way, however. Careful planning is essential to good parenting and, of course, a good parent must be aware of concerns about the future but there is a difference between healthy planning and panicking and willingly riding the mental and emotional "rollercoaster of dread."

A final fear that parents/caregivers of children diagnosed with AS/HFA must get rid of is the fear of judgment from others. I talk with many parents who are afraid to take their children out in public because "what will people think if he acts out?" My response is this: "Who cares?" I do believe that we are responsible to teach our children appropriate social behavior and I do know that children diagnosed with AS/HFA sometimes display behavior that is not socially acceptable, but most of the people we worry about offending are complete strangers we will probably never see again. Our culture is full of double standards and hypocrisy and two unrealistic expectations are that children should be "perfect," and families should be "normal." There is no "perfect" child and no one knows what "normal" is; yet the pressure is on for parents to make sure everything looks okay on the outside which usually comes at the sacrifice of substantive relationships between parents and their children. I tell parents and caregivers of children diagnosed with AS/HFA they better create a thicker "skin" and get used to the stares and comments of ignorant, judgmental strangers and family members. I also tell them that through the experience of having a child diagnosed with AS/HFA they will find out who really loves them and who is willing to stay connected when the going gets tough. I teach them to say the following in a kind but firm manner, "My child and I need love and encouragement; if you are willing to provide that please help me and join us in this tough and amazing journey. If not, please keep your comments to yourself." One mother told me, "I said that to my friend and she has not called me in months." Enough said.

BE A CHEERLEADER!

Parents and caregivers of a child diagnosed with AS/HFA must be cheerleaders for their child. A cheerleader is someone who can give encouragement and look for the positive in every situation, seeking to turn even the most negative circumstances into positive ones. Modeling positive, socially acceptable behavior plays a very large role in helping shape the child's thinking, and when the child is in a positive, social, loving environment it will pay dividends. The problem for many parents of children diagnosed with AS/HFA is that they are tired. Many parents and caregivers are simply "worn out" and are stuck in survival mode, existing from day to day and lacking the energy that it takes to be a cheerleader. However, I tell parents and caregivers that adopting a cheerleader role is not about jumping around and conducting huge celebrations at every turn. That would be ridiculous and probably do more harm than good.

What I am talking about is using words of encouragement, words of hope, and positive actions that create an atmosphere of safety and positive energy that pulls both the parent and the child out of mere "survival mode" to real living and growing. The first thing parents have to do is change their vocabulary. Try to pay attention to the words you use each day and you will understand what I am talking about. Most people use words that are negative in nature when describing their experiences or themselves. Such as "disaster," "terrible," "horrible," "catastrophe," "worst," "never," and "always" just to name a few. They use phrases such as "It is a huge mess," "epic failure," "lost cause," and "worst day ever". These words and phrases are triggers that zap our energy and put our brains into "fight-or-flight" mode. By eliminating these words from our vocabulary and switching to more positive, truth-based descriptions, we save our energy, our children learn better coping skills, and our relationship stays intact.

Please do not think I am encouraging parents to shift into denial mode and put on a "happy face" and simply stuff all the negative thoughts and emotions. You have probably been doing that for a long time, and in fact that would do more harm than good and your child will see right through it. What I am saying is to adopt words and phrases that are truth based and more positive in nature such as "Challenge" instead of "disaster;" "This is a tough day," instead of "This is the worst day ever;" "I am really tired today" instead of "I am the worst parent on the face of the earth." Being a cheerleader incorporates the attributes of patience and being non-reactive. It sends the message that we as parents are confident, in control, positive, and that love is unconditional. When we are tired, we admit that. When we are frustrated we can put that into words, too. However, we communicate that it is the situation or circumstances that we are frustrated with not the child. We continue to find ways to build up, teach, and encourage no matter what.

I worked with a mother of a six year old child diagnosed with AS/HFA who came to me for help and she told me that the morning routine at their house was "complete chaos;" each morning was an "utter failure," and so on because of the difficulty in getting the child ready for school. The child hated certain types of clothing and socks and shoes and would struggle, fight, kick and tantrum, but on the other hand, hated being late to school. Thus, the child's resistance caused him to be late, but he did not see that part of it and would instead blame his mom and become angry with her. Some of you reading this will no doubt identify with opposite extremes such as this. She told me that since the child was a toddler every day was a "wrestling match" and she would gather the clothes in one hand and the child in the other and begin this process which may take anywhere from ten to thirty minutes and by the end the mother was exhausted, angry, and usually in tears and the child was somehow energized from the encounter. I helped her see that the themes behind this routine for the child were power and control, reassurance of love, physical release of frustration, and routine. Since this had gone on for over four years, part of him assumed that this is the role that he is supposed to play.

By helping her adopt a positive, solution-focused approach, she was able to shape his behavior and pull herself out of the wrestling match role and gradually moved him towards getting himself dressed. Encouragement was a key part of this, cheering him on and guiding him through the process. She explained that she could no longer fight and that he would have to help her, but as soon as he got out of control she would have to walk away. She was able to stay non-reactive and was able to communicate through her frustration when things did not go well ("Wow, we are having a tough morning today. Some days are just a challenge aren't they?") but she did not lose control. As she gradually did less and less for him she would cheer him ("C,mon! You can do it! Yes! Very good! Wow, you are doing so well!"). Soon he was able to get himself dressed and she provided reassurance of her love without the physical fight and she was able to turn that into positive touch through holding him and reading to him before school.

"Just Be"

I do a lot of relationship building work with couples and families, and one concept that I teach to parents and couples alike is "just be." "Just Be" implies that I want nothing or expect anything, and I am not forcing any piece of myself onto anyone else. I am simply here. Right here, right now. It also sends the message that I am a blank slate for another person to write on, a blank canvas to be painted upon. I am teachable, moldable, and able to listen and absorb. Many parents/caregivers are so used to "doing" that they forget the "being" part of relationship. When our children are small we are the ringleader, supervisor, activity manager, chef, costume designer, set and backdrop manager, and maid. I tell parents to shift out of this and "just be." This is a very important part of building relationship with children diagnosed with AS/HFA because these children tend to be very strong gatekeepers of who they let in their little worlds. Should someone try too hard, he will find the gates firmly locked. Should someone assume they are guaranteed access because of who she is (for example, mom) she will be shut out and sorely disappointed. No, building relationship with a child diagnosed with AS/HFA is usually by invitation only, and unless parents or caregivers surrender and allows themselves to "just be," the child will not feel safe enough to allow them to be a part of the process.

Parents of children diagnosed with AS/HFA often say "My child won't talk to me. How am I supposed to connect with him?" This is when I share with them the concept of "just be" and tell them to plunk down next to the child who is playing video games, or the kid who draws for hours and hours. I tell parents to soak up everything the child is into and research the music, TV shows, movies, toys, or whatever interests that the child has. I remind the parent that despite the large emphasis our culture places on verbal communication, it is only a small piece of relationship building, especially with individuals diagnosed with AS/HFA. I have learned (sometimes the hard way) in my therapy sessions that my presence is powerful and communicates a great deal. I have very little time to form a connection and if I send the message that I have an agenda and fire questions at the person, more than likely he or she will shut down and the therapeutic bond will not be formed.

The parent/caregiver must remember that for many children diagnosed with AS/HFA, it is hard for them to put feelings into words. When asking a question, be patient and wait for an answer. If, after a time, an answer does not come, try changing the question and ask it in a different way. There are very few situations in which we as parents/caregivers need a question answered immediately; it is our impatience and desire for control that usually drives the process. I worked with one young man who taught me the power of patience and to truly "just be." Early in our meetings I would ask him questions and he would not respond to them. I assumed that he just did not care and I would ignore it and move on to another topic. Finally, in frustration he said to me, "I am going to answer your questions if you would wait!" He then proceeded to answer several of the questions and he explained to me that when he was asked a question, his brain thought of every response for each question and "over-analyzed" the purpose of the question which explained why it took so long. This revelation not only helped build our relationship, but also helped me work with him on reducing the "over-analyzing" which sped up his ability to answer a question and also improved his ability to better connect with others.

Be Consistent and Predictable

Parents/caregivers of children diagnosed with AS/HFA need to be consistent in providing structure and routine and be predictable in the way that they handle the emotional outbursts of their child and their own emotional "stuff." Perhaps one of the greatest disruptive influences that undermine a parent's ability to build relationship is inconsistency. When a child does not know what is coming and cannot predict how a parent/caregiver may react in a certain situation, the "fight-or-flight" response begins to escalate in the child. Human beings naturally feel the urge to avoid people or situations that are not predictable, and children diagnosed with AS/HFA tend to respond positively to a consistent routine. Because these children tend to go into "fight-or-flight" quite easily, the parents/caregiver's ability to control their own emotional reactions in a predictable manner help the child maintain a sense of safety. When bedtimes, mealtimes, and other events in the home are at a set time each day, it helps the child feel secure. When the parent handles an emotional outburst of the child in the same way and does not lose control, it adds to the child's sense of security. When a parent/caregiver provides consequences for poor choices in the same way each time, the child's sense of security remains intact.

In order to grasp the importance of this, we must remember the brain discussion from earlier. Remember that I explained how when an individual is in "fight-or-flight" mode the frontal lobes shut off? Well this is significant when we think about the learning process, because in order to learn something we must be able to access our short-term and long-term memory as well as the ability to concentrate; this is all housed in the frontal lobe area. It is nearly impossible to learn anything when in "fight-or-flight" mode! This is why I stress over and over to parents to never try and reason with an emotional child, and also why I encourage parents to wait until they are calm and the child is calm before having any "heavy" discussions. By being consistent and predictable, the parent lays the groundwork for a calm, peaceful, environment that helps to provide the child with a sense of safety and security which allows the child to grow and learn. This is also powerful in building relationship because trust is directly related to feeling secure and a sense of security is directly related to consistency and predictability.

Consistency is not only important in routine, discipline, and handling emotional situations, but it is important in giving praise, showing affection, and giving encouragement. A child's sense of security is solidified when he or she is rewarded for good choices and when the child knows the parent notices even the smallest attempt at making positive, healthy choices. Very often parents ignore the child when he or she are being "good;" and many children learn to believe that to get their parent's attention they have to act out, even though it may bring negative consequences. I try to help parents see that consistency in praise, routine, consequences, and handling emotional situations lays a firm foundation for a child to grow and learn. For the child diagnosed with AS/HFA this sense of security is even more important due to the difficulties that come from AS/HFA which often gives the child the sense that "I am not safe" in many situations and environments. For parents/caregivers seeking to connect with their child, consistency and predictability are very important.

Live in the Miracle of Now

I have come to see children, adolescents, and adults diagnosed with AS/HFA as true miracles. The way these amazing individuals learn, see the world, and interact with the world on their own terms, in completely original ways is actually very refreshing. My journey in working with the children, adolescents, and adults has been an interesting one, full of ups and downs and I do not have the time or space to write all the blessings that I have experienced along the way. But as I think of one characteristic that sums up all that I have written in this chapter, it is this: Live in the miracle of now. Live in the miracle of the way your child diagnosed with AS/HFA thinks; how they smile; how they love. Live in the miracle right now of how it feels to watch him build something or create a scene from a movie; soak in every moment of what it is like to hear her tell about something she loves so much they could talk for a whole year without stopping. Live in the miracle of jumping into play with him, as he directs you and tells you what to do, where to stand, and what to say. Throw away the fear of the future as you live in the miracle of now; throw away the "supposed to's" and the social and cultural expectations; live in the miracle that in this moment, right here right now; nothing else matters but you and your child. Now is all we have, and there are no guarantees about any other days, minutes, or hours, only right now. I know you are tired; I know you are scared. I know because I see you every day in my office. But may I say one more time, live in the miracle of now and truly embrace who your child is and how much of a role you play in helping your young person grow and learn through the connection that is built with you. *Live in the miracle of now!*

CHAPTER 4

Techniques to Build Connection with Children Diagnosed with AS/HFA

The Miracle of Play

I love to play. I play basketball and board games with my own children on a regular basis; I throw and kick balls with the young people who come to my office. I get on the floor and play in the sandbox with children who come to see me, building sand castles, digging tunnels, and making forts for Army men out of sand. I play with Lincoln Logs and Tinker Toys, LEGO®, and Matchbox cars with the children who come to me. I draw and color and paint; I build with Play Doh and clay. I play computer games and video games with the children and adolescents that are referred to me, defeating the evil Bowser in Super Mario or building a make-believe world in Sims. I play board games often and usually find myself on the losing end of a heated Chess match. I am constantly playing something on my Smart Phone, whether it is a golf game, Words with Friends, or chess (trying to learn some tips to beat these brilliant youngsters!). There is not a day that goes by that I am not doing something surrounding the activity of play. And I love it!

As a boy, I remember sinking into the magic of play and becoming lost for hours in my pretend worlds. Whether I was an explorer discovering a new world in my sandbox, or creating imaginary worlds of pirates, "bad guys", and heroes with my friends, there was something invigorating about play. I remember that it was not just a "fun" thing to do to fill time; I remember that it made my brain feel good too, as well as my body. It turns out, what I was experiencing is the well-documented phenomenon that engaging in play activities encourages brain growth in addition to body growth. I could bore you severely by listing several studies that support the benefits of play not only for children and adolescents, but also for adults. If you are a hungry researcher, the information is out there for you to find. Yes, it is true! Grandma and Grandpa are warding off the effects of dementia by playing a computer game or a round of cards with their friends. Small children are doing much more than just passing the time by digging in the dirt. Just remember this fact: Play is vital for physical, mental, emotional, and social growth in human beings from infancy all the way through the end of the life cycle. Those who engage in some form of play tend to be healthier, mentally sharp, and socially well-adjusted than those who do not engage in regular play. The urge to play is also universal and a naturally occurring phenomenon.

Play and healthy brain development is important to consider when discussing children and adolescents on the autism spectrum. New research on brain development has shed new light on how the brains of children on the autism spectrum seem to get "stuck" in "fight or flight" mode and how play and connection can help stimulate the brain's growth. As I told you earlier, the brain is designed with mechanisms that takes in sights and sounds and quickly decodes those sights and sounds. Once identified as "safe," these mechanisms quickly shift the brain over to "safety mode." For the child on the autism spectrum, however, these mechanisms function differently; noises and stimuli are constantly interpreted as "threatening" and the child's brain stays in "fight or flight" mode. To put it simply, neurotypical individuals have a "brake" that slows or stops the switch in the brain from interpreting something as threatening and helps to prevent the shift of the brain and body into "fight or flight;" but the individual diagnosed with AS/HFA does not. The neurotypical brain has many connections that make the various parts of the brain able to "talk" with one another to decode whether a situation is threatening or not; the brain of the individual on the autism spectrum is left to struggle to make sense of the "data." However, new research is showing that play and connection with others can help form better connections between these parts of the brain.[12] This emerging research highlights the importance of parents and caregivers spending time with their young people diagnosed with AS/HFA in connection through play. It seems that the more the young person on the autism spectrum engages in play and relationship, their brains "learn" to shift over to "safety mode" in a slow, but progressive manner. This is great news for us who work with these young people and also you parents and caregivers!

---

[12] Badenoch, B. & Bogdan, 2012. *Safety and Connection: The Neurobiology of Play.* In *Play-Based Interventions for Children and Adolescents with Autism Spectrum Disorders* (Gallo-Lopez, L. & Rubin, L. C. Editors) New York, NY: Routledge.

My journey into the world of therapeutic play with young people began when I began working at the Florida Baptist Children's Home in Lakeland, Florida in my early twenties. I found that play was very necessary in this work, and I instantly formed bonds with children and adolescents because I could throw a ball, play a video game, or make up silly games outside the cottage after dinner. One of these games stays stuck in my mind: "FruitBall." There were old fruit trees with oranges and grapefruit behind the cottage and we would roll them down the side street that led to a very busy intersection with cars whizzing by at fast speeds on the main road. The goal was to get the fruit to roll through the intersection un-splattered, hopefully reaching the curb on the other side. An orange was five points, a grapefruit was ten. When a car ran over one of the fruits, especially a grapefruit the sight and sound was magnificent and we would all cheer and "ooh and ahh" like we were watching fireworks. Sometimes we would have water balloon fights. Sometimes we would just throw acorns at things like signs or poles. Kids wanted to talk with me and spend time with me; I did not know at the time that my playful spirit made them feel safe and that I was able to be trusted. The experience at the Children's Home in Lakeland was powerful; so powerful that I made psychology and counseling my major and was determined to go as far as I could go to learn as much as I could about helping kids and families.

A few years later while working at a local community health center I attended a training on play therapy and another burst of creative and imaginative energy washed over me as I realized what I had known all along: Play is necessary for humans to engage in; play is important in forming relationships; and play can be used to help heal and teach. Play induces laughter, provides distance from things that are too harsh or scary, and helps us look at the world in a different way. Play brings a rush of happiness and joy that we never want to end; it is like hanging on to those last few minutes of daylight and soaking up every single second of a day because it was so great you can't bear for it to end. Play makes older people feel young again; play brings a rush of memories and happy, fuzzy feelings. Play allows us to find out about ourselves; my brother likes to say that if you play a game with someone you can discover a lot about that person's character and personality. Play makes people feel safe, and most importantly, play builds relationship.

Therapeutic/Developmental Benefits of Play

I decided to include this section because I want the parents/caregivers to fully grasp how powerful play is and how important it is in a child's developmental journey. This information is derived from years of psychological inquiry and rigorous research. The basic summary of this information is that play is completely essential for a child's healthy physical, mental, emotional, and I believe, spiritual development. To be deprived of the ability to play is similar to locking a child in a room and not giving them social contact, food, or water. It would be akin to living without limbs; or trying to function without the ability to see or touch. Play is so much more than just something kids do in between school and sleeping; it is the breath of life for children and provides a way for them to learn about themselves and the world around them. It is also a powerful tool for parents in that by connecting with their child through play they have the ability to teach, communicate, and love.

Teaching and Learning

Play creates valuable teaching and learning experiences. The opportunity is available for the parent (or any other adult) to teach the child through the play experience. I often use LEGO® figures, or dolls to show appropriate social behavior. I have also used games like Chess or Checkers to teach decision making skills for children and adolescents with impulse control problems. Many children I work with are bullied and have very low self-worth as a result of the bullying. Through play they express their thoughts and feelings regarding the bullying, and then use LEGO® figures or puppets to act out appropriate responses to the bullying. They are also able to switch roles and be the bully which is helpful for them to understand that the bully is an insecure person who does not like who he or she is. Video games are also very useful because these games have themes of working together, not giving up, and using good impulse control to reach a goal. For children struggling behaviorally in school, I use video games as a metaphor for walking through their day and ignoring those things that will impede their progress, and focusing on making good choices that will help them reach their goals.

Sharing Thoughts and Feelings

Play allows the opportunity for children to express their thoughts and feelings. Most adults think of play simply as "something fun" they did when they were young, but think back to your play experiences. What feelings do you remember experiencing?

Most will remember a wonderful feeling that was associated with the activity, a sense of calm and peace. Do you remember being very upset about something but after your play experience you felt better? This is what drew us to the activity and why we did not want to stop. The use of play in my work is invaluable because children (and especially individuals diagnosed with AS/HFA) have a hard time putting into words what they feel and think. Play is the vehicle that does this for them. For example, one young boy was having a lot of fear because his father was a violent man and his parents divorced because of it. His play had themes of safety. Whether it was playing in the sandbox or building with LEGO® he was always making his imaginary world "safe." He would make escape helicopters, hidden passageways, and booby traps just in case "the bad guys came". It was impossible for him to tell me, "My dad gets really mad and yells and breaks things, so I try to make myself feel as safe as possible whenever I can." But it was revealed in his play and after he made something that helped his characters feel safe, he would feel safe also. Through this play I was able to boost his sense of safety and help him not go into "panic mode" but instead to stop, look around, and remind himself that he was "O.K." and that Dad was getting help for his anger problem.

RELIVING, AND REPLAYING STRESSFUL EVENTS

Play allows a child to re-live something that was painful or scary. This is very healthy in the fact that when we are in "fight-or-flight" mode, the part of our brain that puts words and meaning to the experience is not working very well. Thus, the memory of the experience brings up a great deal of negative emotions leaving the person feeling very unsteady. This is what is known as Post-traumatic Stress (PTSD) and trauma work helps take little pieces of the trauma and put words to the scary pictures and make meaning of the experience. When the child plays out the traumatic event, the child is in control of the experience which helps his or her their brain "reprocess" the experience in a safe manner and enables the child to view the unpleasant event from an emotionally safe distance.

Over the years, I have used play to help children re-enact situations in which the child was abused, abandoned, or involved in a domestic dispute. I worked with one girl whose parents were divorcing. Like many children, she came to believe that it was her fault (many children choose this option because at younger ages the child sees each parent as perfect and is afraid to assign any blame to either one or both). Through playing out the scenarios with dolls and stuffed animals, she was able to see things from her parent's point of view. At one point in the play, she used a Ken and Barbie doll to represent her parents and she played out various arguments that she remembered between her parents. Through this play she was able to see that it was more about them not getting along, not about her at all. She was also able to see that her parents could remain friends and work together (which they did) and that she would still get to see them. She realized that what was so uncomfortable about divorce was the unknown; her life had been pretty predictable up to that point and not knowing what was coming was really frightening.

Instilling a Sense of Control

Play allows a child to be in control. Most children's lives consist of being told what to wear, where to go, and how to act, and play is a wonderful escape from the demands of adults. This is what is becoming scarce in our society today. Our busyness is being forced upon our children so that when we see them with "downtime" we think that there is something wrong. As a result, many children are being put into so many activities and programs that they are developing severe physical, emotional, and mental strain from the pressure of being too busy. It is important for a child and adolescent to have "downtime;" especially when it comes to free play. Free play allows a child to have a sense of: "I'm in charge;" "I get to say what happens;" "I am the boss!" This gives the child a chance to experiment, learn, and practice being in control which helps emotional and mental development. A sense of control is important as it aids in the child learning to self-soothe and build up a healthy self-worth. When children engage in free play, they are able to feel good about themselves and understand their sense of value and worth.

Healthy Sense of Attachment

Play helps build connection! Playing with your child is one of the sure ways to build a deep, long-lasting relationship and to reassure your child that he or she is loved and cared for. A well-known fact in the field of psychology is that a strong sense of attachment is essential to healthy mental and emotional growth and development. When children are bonded with a parent they know is not going to leave them or stop loving them, there are parts of his or her brain, emotions, personality, and physical self that are free to grow. By playing with our children, we send the message that "You are important;" "I think you are valuable;" and "I think you are special." As children grow into adolescents and on into adulthood, that healthy sense of attachment is what gives them the courage to make friends, try new things, and eventually go out on their own. Play is one of the key factors in giving this sense of attachment to our children.

I have worked with several children over the years that have been abandoned, rejected, or ignored by various caregivers. One of the most powerful things I have witnessed in using play therapy with these children is how much play serves as a way for them to communicate about their feelings and give meaning to what they are sensing. One little guy and I were playing in the sand box where he loved to make battle scenes and have wars. He had an "on-again-off-again" relationship with his father and had a lot of emotional issues related to the consistent rejection which resulted in problems in school and at home with his mother. Play therapy was powerful for him and provided a release of the emotions and being able to talk about his father. He felt safe with our relationship because he knew that he could say and do anything in the therapy room and not be punished for it. Over time, his emotional issues began to disappear and a strong, confident, kind young man began to emerge. One day he surprised me as we played in the sand. He was building a mountain and digging a tunnel underneath. When he completed it, he stepped back and beamed with pleasure at the creation he had made. Then he blurted out "I don't need my dad in my life for me to know that I am valuable and loveable! He is missing out on time with me, but that is his choice! When he is ready he will spend time with me, and I don't really want to be around him if he doesn't really want me and that is okay." I was stunned by his revelation, as well as the power of play in helping heal emotional pain and building self-worth and self-confidence. The key however, was in our relationship that laid the foundation for him to feel safe, free to play and explore, and verbalize his thoughts and feelings.

PLAY REMOVES DEFENSIVE WALLS AND BARRIERS

Play usually equals fun, and when human beings are having fun, they usually let down protective emotional walls and barriers that they use to keep inner thoughts and feelings hidden. Children are no different, and when parents engage in play with their child, they often report that they are shocked at how open the child is with them, and many parents tell me that they find out how the child feels about death, friends, and even sex from time spent in play with the child. It is important to remember that two different internal states cannot exist together. For instance, it is impossible to be relaxed and anxious, or depressed and playful at the same time. It has to be one or the other. Play helps the negative emotional states (i.e. fear, sadness, frustration) lessen and boosts the areas of the brain such as problem solving which leads to better coping skills, which leads to positive emotional states like happiness and joy. This helps explain why many children who appear restless and who get in trouble for "playing too much" are often simply trying to soothe negative emotions they are feeling, but teachers and pediatricians diagnose these children with ADHD and put them on medications which is the last thing the child needs.

I worked with one young boy who was "coming out of his skin" according to his mother. He was scratching himself obsessively, and exhibited emotional meltdowns over seemingly insignificant things. Upon meeting with him, I immediately identified that he became easily overwhelmed by negative emotions (fear and frustration) which resulted in anger that cycled back to fear and frustration. It was classic "fight-or-flight" which is common in individuals diagnosed with AS/HFA. I used play to help him be able to tolerate negative emotions in small doses. One of the forms of play that I used was video games. Some of the games he knew and was quite good at playing, but I began to use games that he did not know. I do this often with children and adolescents who have difficulty tolerating negative emotions. This young man would begin to get frustrated and we could pause the game, take some deep breaths, and re-focus. By doing this over and over, he gradually could step closer and closer to these emotions that used to baffle him and send him into maximum emotional overdrive. I then helped him see that real life situations that caused him to be frustrated were no different than a new level on a video game and taught him a new pathway in his brain. Instead of choosing to be reactive, he could choose emotional control and reap the rewards of good choices.

Using Play to Building Connection between Parents and Children Diagnosed with AS/HFA

We come now to the "meat" of the book. What follows are some ideas and suggestions for you to connect and build deeper connections with your child. I want to remind parents/caregivers that what works for one child/family may not work for another; remember to not allow discouragement and despair to set in. Do not give up!

Use Your Child's Specified Interest

What does your child love? Why does he love it? What is it about that activity, toy, or medium that drives her and excites her? In my work, I have to figure these things out rather quickly, and once I do, I zero in on that interest and dissect it in a very short amount of time in order to build connection with the child; I then use my understanding of the interest in order to begin helping the child overcome whatever challenges he or she is experiencing. By spending some time analyzing your child's natural passion for something, you can find ways to connect with your child through that toy or activity. This builds connection in a couple of ways. One, it sends the message that you are present and willing to enter the child's world. A second way that it builds connection is that it provides a pathway for deeper understanding. By sitting and joining in the play, you are able to learn how your child approaches new situations, deals with fear, and how he or she views the world. Very valuable information! Some parents may let out a groan at this point! "You mean I have to sit and listen to him go on and on about his imaginary planet? I already have to hear about it for hours and hours! Do you mean I now am supposed to sit with him and join in, I can barely stand listening to it on the car ride home from school?" My answer is always "YES!" However, I help parents/caregivers learn to save their energy and shift their mindset from a need to "fix" or "endure it" mode to a "just be" mode. I also remind parents/caregivers that they can set limits on how much they get involved in the activity with their child. For instance, setting a timer and only giving their child thirty minutes here or there is a wonderful way to teach the child how to transition and also presents the child with boundaries. Children diagnosed with AS/HFA can be intense and the parents or caregivers often report feeling like they are having "the life sucked out" of them! The last thing they want to do is enter into an activity with their child they perceive is mundane and pointless. However, this is where I help them change their perspective!

One single mother told me about an imaginary world that her son created. It was similar to Pokémon, but even more detailed. She told me how he begged her to play with him and she often would, but said that he could lose himself in the play for hours and hours. My first response was "That is so beautiful," which caught her by surprise. I elaborated on my response by saying that in her description of her son and his play, I saw the wonder and beauty of a child who could completely lose himself in a world that in his mind was as real as the chairs she and I were sitting on. I also told her about the fleeting days of childhood that would someday be gone and how short this time with her son really is; that time never stops marching and the very things that can annoy us as parents will one day be fuzzy, distant, warm, yet untouchable memories. I also explained through joining him in the play she could gather much information and teach him about many things through the play. She could introduce topics such as fear, pain, worry, death; she could teach kindness, sharing, friendship, and so many other character building qualities. I told her the idea about setting the timer and setting limits for her involvement in the play to avoid burnout. She said to me "Thanks for this. I never saw it that way!"

Parental Resistance to the Child's Specified Interest

I often encounter parents of children diagnosed with AS/HFA who are resistant to the idea of joining with their child in the specified interest. The parent's fear is that this will encourage the child in the specified interest and the child will not branch out to other interests. While this resistance of the parent may sound cruel to some people, you must remember the intensity factor that I discussed earlier. I mentioned before how these children can become consumed by what they enjoy. I have observed firsthand in the therapy office where I literally could not get one word into the conversation while a child was involved in what he loved, and when I did the child treated me as if I did not exist and I remember feeling insignificant and lost as I tried to relate to the child. So, when I am at the bridge building stage with parents I let them know that I understand their concerns. I do not want you to think that the parents I encounter are cold or unloving. It is not that these parents do not love their child; in fact, in their defense, they love them enough to try and limit their child's specified interest to help them become well-rounded in their interests. These parents hope that by limiting the interest, the child will be able to better develop mentally, emotionally, and socially. However, I have found by entering into the world of the specified interest of these children, I am able to build relationships with them.

I offer some reassurance to the parents I meet who have these concerns, and I want to offer some to you as well, if you fall into this category. First, trying to break your child of his specified interest is probably going to be very difficult, if not impossible. Children diagnosed with AS/HFA do not think the way we do, and for them, their specified interest is often tied to something that soothes them emotionally. It is like a big cycle: They like it because it brings them comfort, which reinforces how much they like it. I mentioned earlier how the brain of the individual diagnosed with AS/HFA tends to be like one big track with one lane; neurotypical individuals tend to have six or eight lanes. Remember, this does not mean that these individuals are not as intelligent or gifted; in fact, having one lane can often create amazing talent and knowledge in that certain area. For neurotypical folks like us, our brains tend to naturally focus on more than one thing, and even when we do have one interest that we can focus on for a great deal of time, we still go to work, spend time with family, and so on.

I met a father who was concerned about his son's obsession with drawing. He told me that his son drew constantly and never went without his drawing pad and pencils. This obsession had caused difficulties at school, where he would draw on the corners of assignments, books, and papers. He was quite popular with peers as a result of his obsession because he could draw the cartoon characters and video game characters that his peers liked, but it was disruptive for the boy's teacher when this occurred during class time. When we were discussing building a closer connection to his son, I suggested that Dad draw with his son, and this is when he brought up his concerns. He told me about his attempts to curb the interest in drawing which were unsuccessful. He told me how he and his wife took away the drawing as a consequence, which seemed to work for a time, but the boy would ultimately return to it. Like all the parents I work with, I asked him, "What are you afraid of?" His main fear was the one-dimensionality that characterized much of his son's functioning: One interest (drawing), one type of food (pasta), one type of clothing, one friend, one, one, one and so on. I worked to help him see this is not necessarily a bad thing and that children often go through phases with their interests. I reminded him that while it can be exasperating, if his son's obsession was not the drawing it would probably be something else. The father went on to tell me that he and the boy's mother had accepted this was not going to change, but it concerned them at the same time. I encouraged the father join his son in the drawing activity as a way to strengthen the relationship, and since Dad was a "techie," to look for ways to expand the interest into a "real-world" application, such as branching into computer graphics and computer animated drawing.

Second, it is impossible for any of us to know how our children are going to turn out, and what opportunities and choices await them. Think of yourself and the career in which you currently work. Did you methodically plan out where you would be at this point? If you did, were there not some twists and turns you did not foresee? How involved were your parents in your career planning process? My point is that for most of us, we sort of make our path as we go, and even if we went to college or a technical school for specialized training, there are still opportunities and circumstances we did not anticipate. So why do we expect so much out of our children? I am passionate about this because I encounter many discouraged parents who believe their child is going to "jeopardize" the future because of not getting a high enough grade, or missing out on a service opportunity that could earn them a credit or two towards a high school diploma. And these kids are in middle school! The cultural climate has shifted to putting more pressure than ever on our young people to "make it," yet what is missing is relationship. Parents assume technology will do the job, or that schools will magically fill in the gaps. The tough truth is that relationship provides a context for learning and development. Our job is to connect with our children and meet their physical and emotional needs and provide them with opportunities to learn and grow, but we cannot choose their path for them. There are special circumstances, and I do believe children and adolescents with special needs require extra support as they near college and career age, but their choice for a career remains theirs alone.

A third reassurance that I offer to parents is that the specified interest of the child will often result in the child branching out to other interests. For instance, a child who likes the intricate components of LEGO® may go from that to the realm of electronics or building components, which in turn will lead them to the career of architect, electrician, or electric engineer. A young person who is consumed by a video game is amazed by the detail and intricate patterns of the story and how the game works could develop an interest in designing computer systems and programming, or working in a career that relies heavily on computers. As I mentioned earlier, our cultural climate has parents believing that a child should have many "specialties" (sports, art, music, etc.) and that allowing a child to find something he or she loves and delves into is somehow wrong and damaging to the child because the child might be missing out on something. I enjoy reading biographies and autobiographies and one thing that continues to astound me is how people end up in the careers in which they work. A common thread in all of the stories is that relationship was an important ingredient in providing a foundation for learning and growth. From athletes to the "techies," and from musicians to business moguls, they all had people and key individuals that provided a foundational platform of love and encouragement that gave these individuals the inner strength to explore, risk, and grow. I try to communicate to parents of children diagnosed with AS/HFA to not panic and to not form a "gloom and doom" picture of their child's future. The first step in this is to not compare your child with another; instead, to build relationship with your child and seek to know and understand your child.

Toys

Many of us remember a favorite toy. What was yours? For me, I remember the sleekness of a model railroad Amtrak engine and listening to how quietly it ran on the tracks. I still have that engine and it still works. Can you think of a toy that kept you occupied for hours and hours? I ask these questions because I think it is important to drift back and think of what it felt like to have a toy that consumed our interests, and to remember getting lost with a toy that we wanted to play with over and over. These memories provide us with a sense of understanding when our children are consumed with a toy. For parents who have children diagnosed with AS/HFA, toys represent a way to build connection with their child. I will discuss some of the toys that I use in my work with children and describe how each can be a powerful tool in building connection.

BUILDING TOYS:
LEGO®, Lincoln Logs, Tinker Toys and Other Building Toys

Toys that are designed for building are powerful in the hands of children. Children are able to create something that is theirs alone, and the toys I listed above are able to be modified by these children. Building toys are also powerful teaching tools and can be used to help the child learn valuable adaptive skills and problem solving skills through changing and rebuilding a structure. A structure can also represent safety for the child and I have had many children in my practice build structures that represent a safe haven from the chaos in which they live on a regular basis. Another wonderful characteristic of these toys is they are perfect for joining with the child and building something together. Parents are often amazed when they join with their child in building something and find not only the joy of creating something but realize they have bonded with their child in a new way.

LEGO® has a wonderful history and has been making toys since 1934. Children diagnosed with AS/HFA tend to be drawn to the design and function of LEGO® as well as the system-oriented characteristics. LEGO® is orderly, neat, and crisp. They can be moved around, interchanged, and built to any form that one can imagine. LEGO® sets continue to become more and more elaborate and sets have been adapted to the latest movie themes such as LEGO® Star Wars and LEGO® Harry Potter. While sets can be expensive, there are many non-themed sets that can be found for reasonable prices. In addition, sets can be interchanged to make completely new creations. LEGO® also has characters and figures that are part of the LEGO® world, which creates another dimension to the play because the child can use the figures as representation of other people. This can be very valuable with children diagnosed with AS/HFA because it can give the parent the opportunity to teach social skills and help the child begin to see things from another person's perspective. I mentioned earlier what a struggle mindblindness can be for an individual diagnosed with AS/HFA and can cause a great deal of problems in social relationships.

Lincoln Logs and Tinker Toys are toys that older generations of people are sure to remember. Before the days of precision plastics and computers and video games, these glorious wooden toys entertained children for generations. I have found that children of today find these wooden toys fascinating and enjoy using their imaginations to make all sorts of structures and creations. Much like LEGO®, Lincoln Logs and Tinker Toys are precise and have many interlocking pieces and parts. Each comes with a "guide" that teaches the user how to make many different structures, but there is also the option of creating completely unique structures and creations simply by using one's imagination.

So you may ask, "How do I build connection with my child diagnosed with AS/HFA through building toys?" Well, the first step is simply "just be" that I mentioned earlier in the book. Next, allow yourself to simply be in the presence of your child and just watch as they begin to build and arrange the pieces of the building materials. Join in play with your child by picking up some of the building materials and show that you are willing to be a part of the play process. Ask your child if she wants your help and ask her what you should build and how you should help her. If your child only wants to build alone, simply acknowledge that you heard their request and sit back and watch. Ask him about what he is building and watch him create before your eyes. The power in this form of play is that by building together you are creating a metaphor of building a relationship. With each piece put together, you are putting a memory in the mind of your child and sending the message that you care. One of the biggest misconceptions about children diagnosed with AS/HFA is that the child does not want connection with others, particularly parents. This however, is not true at all and I have many children diagnosed with AS/HFA tell me they wish that their parents played with them and showed more of an interest in what they enjoy.

TOY FIGURES:
Army Figures, LEGO® Figures, Dolls, and Other Characters

Toy figures are also powerful in the hands of children because it is through these characters that children play out relationship themes and demonstrate how they see people, giving others a snapshot of what relationships look like through the child's eyes. When I use play therapy with a child that involves toy figures, especially those diagnosed with AS/HFA, I can learn a great deal from how the child uses the toys. For instance, a child can reveal how they view relationships with peers, family members, and even pets. One young boy diagnosed with AS would always line up LEGO® soldiers against each other "so they could fight," "Why do they want to fight?" I asked, after watching several different scenarios. "They just do" he responded. "Everybody always wants to fight." Over and over, he always got the soldiers ready to "fight." This boy exhibited significant difficulties in getting along with others and perceived others as threatening and that "no one likes me." He could not see that he appeared angry, aloof, and sometimes threatening to others, making them cautious to get close to him. This further made him see people as threatening and "mean." Through the play process, I was able to better understand the level of perceived threat this boy felt when he was around others and began to help him change his thinking through a shared play experience.

For parents with girls diagnosed with AS/HFA, dolls represent a wonderful way to teach nurturing and empathy, as well as build connection through modeling. I worked with a mother who was frustrated with being unable to connect with her daughter and often felt like an "outsider" when it came to her relationship with her daughter. Like any mother, she craved affection from her little girl. One thing I encouraged this mother to do was to tell her daughter the story of how she came about. Her daughter was very logical and black and white and was naturally interested in science and the biological/physiological process of living things. She was aware enough to know that mothers carried babies in their stomachs, but like most children was not aware of the nurturing process of the mother. Using a doll, this mother showed her daughter how a mother nurtures, protects, feeds, and cares for a baby and reinforced how fragile and helpless a human baby is. "This is how I held you," she would say, "This is how I fed you," and so on. The little girl was fascinated as her mother told her the story of her getting sick, crying and needing to be comforted, and how her mother carried her everywhere when she was a baby. The young girl began to model her mother's behavior, pretending to nurture and care for a baby through playing with a doll and this process of play helped in building connection between herself and her mother.

Parents can use any type of toy figure to help build connection with their child. While children diagnosed with AS/HFA do not always engage in pretend play, I have noticed that many children will use toy figures to act out various scenes from movies or TV shows. I suggest that if the child is not already drawn to a type of toy figure, then the parent can introduce some and see what happens. Usually, children will incorporate these types of toys quickly into their play sequences and the parents can join in the play simply by grabbing a figure and pretending to act out a scene. If the child does not want the parent to join, then the parent can simply "just be" and watch what happens. By being available and willing to join in the play with toy figures, the parent can not only build better connection but also reach a new level of understanding about their child.

One boy I worked with who was diagnosed with AS/HFA was passionate about Star Wars. His parents were both concerned he would not relate to them and both desperately desired to connect with him. I pointed out to them some of the characteristics of Star Wars and that many of the characters had good character traits. I reminded them that while they did not care much for Star Wars, their child did and it was an opportunity to connect with him through his specified interest. The father told me that he was able to find some used Star Wars figures at a Goodwill Store and said he was going to give them to his son. What happened was nothing short of miraculous as the boy was overjoyed with the toy figures and prompted the father to join in the play as his father made himself available to do so. Both parents also began watching the movies and TV shows and picked up on several themes they were able to use with their son in not only building connection but also learning about how their son saw the world. As he got older, the parents found better ways to relate to him by making the situation similar to scenes from the Star Wars movies and continued to play them out with him using toy figures. I showed the parents how many of the characters found in Star Wars were relatable to teaching social skills and assessing social situations. This is just one more example of how a specified interest is very powerful in building connection between a parent or parents and a child diagnosed with AS/HFA.

Stuffed Animals and Puppets

STUFFED ANIMALS

Did you have a favorite stuffed animal when you were a child? Do you remember not wanting to go anywhere without it? Many of us remember having a stuffed animal that became worn out from years of being slept with and dragged everywhere we went because it represented safety and gave us a sense of security. I usually find that children diagnosed with AS/HFA have a favorite stuffed animal. Stuffed animals have many benefits for young children and give the parents a wonderful tool with which to connect with their child through play. The following section discusses some of the benefits of stuffed animals.

A SUBSTITUTION/TRANSITION OBJECT

Stuffed animals are known as a substitution/transitional object because the object (stuffed animal) can provide the child with a sense of safety and security when the parent is not present, thus it becomes a *substitute object* for the absent parent. This is important for the child's emotional and mental development because the parent cannot be with the child constantly as he or she grows, and future success of the child demands that the child be able to move towards being independent from the parent. Stuffed animals are also known as a *transition object* because the children are able to build up their sense of safety and self-confidence through the object (stuffed animal) when the parent is unavailable, such as when the child goes to grandma's house, school, or sleeps alone. Over time, the child usually matures emotionally, mentally, and physically and is able to self-soothe and does not need the stuffed animal, just as the child does not need as much from the parent as the maturation process takes place.

A CONSTANT COMPANION

A stuffed animal can also represent a companion for a child. When no other play-mates are available, or if the child is very particular in whom he wants to play with (as many children diagnosed with AS/HFA tend to be), the stuffed animal can be the perfect substitute for the child to interact with and give the child a sense of companionship. The stuffed animal sits where the child wants it to sit, and never judges, criticizes, and never does mean things. The child can also practice interacting with the stuffed animal which can build important social skills that can transfer to real life situations. The companionship provides reassurance, as well as a soothing influence, and also stimulates imaginary play as the child interacts with the stuffed animal in pretend play. I have observed that while many children diagnosed with AS/HFA do not engage in pretend play, many have a stuffed animal that provides companionship which I interpret as an object representing unconditional acceptance. Regardless of how the child diagnosed with AS/HFA *appears*, there is still an innate need for a sense of safety and security. Stuffed animals can provide this.

SELF-AWARENESS

Playing with stuffed animals can provide the child with a sense of self-awareness. Through playing with the animal the child gains insight into what she likes, gets to practice how she talks, and reflects to the toy how she sees the world. The stuffed animal acts as a reflective mirror so to speak, providing the child with information that helps him get in touch with who he is and what he likes, etc. Children begin getting to know themselves very early in their lives and play is one of the ways this process occurs. Playing with stuffed animals allows the child to have interaction with another being, and increases the child's awareness of who she is, what she likes, and who she wants to become. This is very valuable in establishing a sense of self and this sense of self serves to lay a foundation for future milestones such as building a career and establishing relationships.

SELF-WORTH

Along with providing the child with a greater sense of self-awareness, stuffed animal play can also help increase a child's sense of self-worth. I wrote earlier how the stuffed animal represents an object that does not reject, does not judge, and unconditionally accepts the child. This continually sends the message to the child that the child is valuable and worthy of love. This helps explain why children who have been abused find comfort in stuffed animals and why stuffed animals play such an important role in the healing process of children that have been abused, rejected, and abandoned. For children who are in families where they are loved unconditionally and receive messages that they are valuable and worthy, playing with stuffed animals reinforces those messages and these children will play out these themes. This "secondary reinforcement" through playing with stuffed animals helps to build the child's self-worth which is important because so many mental, emotional, and social milestones hinge on the strength of a healthy and solid sense of self-worth.

USING STUFFED ANIMALS IN PLAY WITH CHILDREN DIAGNOSED WITH AS/HFA

Parents of children diagnosed with AS/HFA can use stuffed animals in playing with their child to build deeper connections, teach social skills and explain social situations, as well as teach the child about bonding and unconditional love and acceptance. The same "rules" apply to any situation involving imaginary play: Let your imagination guide you, have fun, and "just be" in the moment with your son or daughter. Throw out expectations and agendas, and immerse yourself in the miracle of play.

BUILDING DEEPER CONNECTIONS, TEACHING SOCIAL SKILLS, MODELING LOVE AND ACCEPTANCE

Stuffed animals can be used by the parent to build a great connection with their child diagnosed with AS/HFA. Building an imaginary world using the stuffed animals allows the parent to connect with their child on a level of demonstrating that parents can shift to the child's level. I worked with one mother who noticed that her son diagnosed with AS/HFA loved stuffed animals and could not get enough of them. I encouraged her to use this as a way to connect with him. Like many adults, she "forgot" how to play and I had to "coach" her in remembering how to immerse herself in imaginary play. She and her son used an old box to make a "house" and then she used the various animals to represent various people such as grandma and grandpa, the postman, the bank teller, etc. and pretended to go through her day. Her son was delighted and each evening they played together for about thirty minutes to an hour. She found that this was a powerful tool in giving her son an idea of what she did all day and even told me that it helped to "decompress" about her job, which was a stressful environment for her. She told me one day she replayed a scenario using the stuffed animals in which she had an argument with her boss. She noticed that when she played it out, she could exaggerate her responses and shift perspectives and found that after she and her son were done playing, the situation did not bother her so much. The connection between herself and her son deepened and both found new ways to communicate feelings and thoughts through the pretend play.

Stuffed animals are great play therapy tools because they can be used to represent people. I often use them in my work to help a child explain their family members and the child's relationship to those people. For example, a child who has a step-parent that the child does not like may find it difficult to talk about the step-parent because most children are not comfortable talking about adults to another adult that they do not know very well. However, children can use a stuffed animal to represent that person and channel their thoughts and feelings through the interaction with the stuffed animal. As I explained earlier, this is why play therapy is so powerful and effective because the child is able to maintain a sense of safety and can approach difficult topics and talk about thoughts and feelings through the activity of play. I worked with a child who was in a blended family and was fearful of his mother's new boyfriend. I laid out stuffed animals and told him we were going to use the stuffed animals to represent his family members and pretend that the stuffed animals were at his mother's house for dinner. The boy picked various stuffed animals to represent his mother, siblings, and other family members. When it came time to pick one to represent his mother's boyfriend he hesitated and then chose a Siberian Husky dog. The themes that emerged from his play with this stuffed animal were that the dog was a bully, loud and obnoxious, bossy, and downright mean. He was able to express his true feelings about the person in a way that was safe for him and provided words and meaning to his feelings about the man.

Children diagnosed with AS/HFA are usually at a loss when dealing with people and social situations. Many parents describe their children diagnosed with AS/HFA as "bystanders" "observers" and "on the sidelines" when talking about how their child approaches social situations. We as parents know that we are "supposed" to teach our children the social games that they will encounter on a daily basis, but most of us are at a loss at how to do this. I remind parents that this occurs through relationship, and the path to relationship is through connecting through play. Stuffed animals are one more way to provide your child with a picture of navigating social situations through pretend play. I used this technique with two parents who were bothered that their son never "joined" in play with other children. He desired to be with other children and would be in the play area but he seemed at a loss in what to do in joining in play. The boy also loved stuffed animals and I instructed the parents to build a social network using the stuffed animals and change the context. For example, one day they might pretend the stuffed animals are at the park, the next time they might be at church, and so on. This allowed for the parents to use the animals and also model how different behavior was appropriate at different times. It not only created tighter bonds with the parents and promoted trust, but it also was a way for the parents to teach valuable social skills.

Finally, play using stuffed animals is a way for the parent to model unconditional love and acceptance to the child diagnosed with AS/HFA. I wrote earlier how stuffed animal toys can be a powerful stabilizing object for the child that positively impacts self-worth and a sense of self. Play that involves stuffed animals between the parent and the child sends the message to the child that the parent is stable, trustworthy, and reflects unconditional love to the child. I instruct parents to choose a stuffed animal that represents a parent figure, like a "mother bear," or a "father penguin." Once this is done, I instruct the parent to create scenarios in which they are able to demonstrate unconditional love and acceptance. For example, a father using a "father penguin" may play out a scenario in which the father penguin protects a young penguin and keeps the young penguin safe. This narrative could change and be restructured based on the issue or issues that relate to the child on the autism spectrum. Through this play, the parent models for the child diagnosed with AS/HFA the characteristics that lay a foundation of trust and confidence.

PUPPETS

Therapists and counselors who work with children usually have puppets in some form on hand because these toys are very useful for a number of reasons. Puppets allow the child to shift roles and pretend to be another person. Puppets allow for the teaching of socially appropriate behavior. Puppets also allow children to share what they are feeling and thinking, but can be done in a fun and safe manner. I have used puppets to help children deal with bullying, the pain of losing a loved one, and even to help them learn valuable social skills. Puppets have been a great tool to help me connect with young people and also find out what a child thinks and feels about an unpleasant subject such as abuse or divorce. Puppets have also helped me teach a child to see a situation from another person's perspective by having them pretend to be someone else through puppet play.

Puppets are valuable when working with children diagnosed with AS/HFA to introduce social skills and to help children learn to share their feelings and thoughts. Many children diagnosed with AS/HFA struggle with putting their thoughts and feelings into words and this causes difficulties in the social arena. Puppets are a way to help children diagnosed with AS/HFA to learn to articulate thoughts and feelings and practice being in a social situation in a fun and safe way. For example, I conduct groups with children diagnosed with AS/HFA and I use puppets to help them practice being in a group and interacting with others. The puppet seems to take away the fear and many children who struggle saying anything will suddenly come alive with a puppet on their hand. I notice the children will also stay in the activity much longer than they would without using the puppet. I also have the children switch puppets and change into another character which they also seem to find fun. One young boy who comes to my office will automatically go to my basket and grab a puppet immediately upon coming to the office and will sometimes keep it on for most of the session. He says that this helps him "talk better." I am gradually getting him to share thoughts and feelings without the puppet, but it has proven to be very useful in helping this boy feel safe in sharing thoughts and feelings.

Using Puppets to Build Bridges

Much like stuffed animals, puppets can be used by parents to build deeper connection with their child diagnosed with AS/HFA while at the same time teaching valuable social skills and building up the child's sense of self-worth. A parent can take a puppet and pretend to be a character and encourage the child to do the same. Through modeling various social interactions, the parent's puppet can take on a number of roles. They can be a teacher, peer, aggressor (bully), or a parent figure. Children, seeing the parent take on a role such as these; can be free to "play" a role that is interesting to them. One parent and child that I worked with ended up acting out Star Wars scenes even though they were using animal puppets such as a pig, cow, and a rooster. The parent told me they became so involved in the play the parent thought they were in Star Wars! This mother had never before seen her son as animated as when they engaged in puppet play, and she later told me it brought her hope for the future and helped calm her fears.

Parents sometimes have to be reminded that children diagnosed with AS/HFA do not always naturally engage in pretend play, so the parent has to be directive in the play. Puppets fall into the imaginary play category and I encourage parents to be directive such as telling the child, "I am going to be the principal, and you are going to be the student;" or "This time you be the bully and I will pretend to be the one who is being bullied." This helps the child know what role to play and is he or she more likely to get involved in the play. This directive role of the parent also serves to provide the child with a sense of safety and gives the parent the opportunity to adopt an authoritative role yet in the context of play. As I wrote earlier, this provides the parent with a wonderful opportunity to help instill a sense of safety and love through leadership and direction in a positive activity (play) and allows the parent to show a different side of the parent's personality.

Another fun activity that a parent can use with puppets is to allow the child to play a dominant role such as a police officer, principal, or parent while the parent plays a submissive role (someone getting a speeding ticket, needing a detention for poor school behavior, or refusing to do chores in the home and going to time out). This "role-reversal" can help children diagnosed with AS/HFA experiment with other roles and help expand their thinking as well as bring out often hidden parts of their personalities. I have even pretended to be a kid coming to counseling and told the child to be the counselor. My puppet talked about having trouble in school, getting bullied, and being sick and tired of being told to load and unload the dishwasher by mom. The child I was working with was absolutely delighted to be the counselor, and relished in telling me that my "bad attitude" and "disrespect" was only making things worse. "What can I do?" my puppet moaned. "My life is so miserable!" The boy's face brightened as his puppet put its little puppet arm around my puppet in an act of comfort. I was stunned. "Don't worry its normal for kids to mess up. Your mom only loves you and that is why she makes you do chores and stuff" he said, as sincere as could be. Through using a puppet to take on different roles, each of us was forced to see things from a different perspective. I challenge parents to engage in role-reversal play often, not just with puppets, to help them see things from their child's eyes and also to get a glimpse of the values that the parents have worked so hard to instill. Because we rarely put our children in a situation to use the values and knowledge we have given them, we often believe our hard work has been wasted and that our children will never "get it." This type of play can reveal valuable feedback information for the parent and provide reassurance that the child has incorporated the parent's values and morals that the parent has worked so hard to instill in the child.

Games (Board, Imaginary, Electronic)

Rachel and Tony

Rachel, a single mom, is playing chess with her ten-year-old son Tony, who was diagnosed with AS/HFA at seven years of age. She agonizes over her next move. If she moves her rook to keep it out of danger, Tony will take her knight, and if she moves her knight out of danger, he will take her rook. She has to figure out which one she can live without. "How do you always do this to me!" she cries with false indignation. Tony squeals with delight at her dilemma. He beams as he once again masterfully concocts her demise. He methodically picks off piece by piece, finally leaving her with only her king and pawn, and toys with her awhile before fully putting her in checkmate. Once this is completed and Rachel has been forced to surrender, Tony jumps up and runs around the room singing "I am the *champion,* my friends!!!" He rushes over and hugs Rachel and asks her if she will play again.

Rachel began playing chess six months ago at the suggestion of Tony's counselor, who said it would be a good way to build connection with Tony. Rachel, like many mothers, felt like a manager of her son and was happy to care for him by cleaning, cooking meals, and picking him up and taking him where he needed to go, but she felt there was something missing. She had grown used to Tony's routines and they both functioned very well together, each doing their own "thing" but she was worried that he saw her as an object that provided him with food and transportation and nothing more. Being a single mother of a son had always worried her because she doubted that she could meet his emotional and mental needs. She knew that in many ways Tony was far beyond her in the intellectual department, and this intimidated her. She began taking Tony for counseling at the suggestion of some of his teachers in order to help him learn to control the emotional outbursts he was beginning to exhibit. Rachel began to notice Tony had started to grow emotionally as a result of the counseling, and had become much more expressive. She talked with the counselor and asked what he did with Tony and the counselor explained how he used play therapy techniques with Tony. The counselor listened as Rachel explained her feelings of sadness and frustration at not being able to connect with Tony and the counselor suggested playing with him for a short time each day. He told her that one of Tony's favorite games was chess and that it would be a great connection builder for her and Tony. The therapist explained that playing a game that Tony loved would change the dynamics in their relationship and would put her in more of a "real person" role instead of the "house manager." He also explained that Chess had many important teaching aspects such as logic and reasoning and social connection. Rachel had not played in years and did not know the correct names for the pieces, which annoyed Tony as she called the knight her "horsey-guy" and called the bishop "pointy-man." But Tony taught her the names and reminded her of some of the moves of the pieces. She noticed that when she let herself be available to him for play that he was quite a teacher and showed a great deal of patience. Soon their Chess matches became a daily ritual and she gradually noticed a shift that occurred in their relationship. She saw pieces of him she had not noticed before, and he began to joke with her and showed more signs of physical affection. Their games of Chess expanded to other games and play activities, such as playing video games together and building with LEGO®. Rachel finally began to feel she was actually a part of his life instead of just a "manager."

Board Games

I use a lot of board games in my work. Board games are powerful in helping form connection because there is a mutual sharing of an experience and the "fun" factor helps to lessen defenses and put people at ease. Board games also help teach a variety of skills from practical learning (math, decision making, etc.) as well as social learning (taking turns, listening to others, etc.). Think back to the board games you played as a child. What themes were present? What did you like about the games? With whom did you play them? For many of us, Monopoly taught us about money, counting, and buying property; LIFE taught us to think about jobs, college, and investing; and SORRY taught us about strategy. I also use board games when helping to rebuild connection within a family, and helping children with deficits in social skills learn about how to connect with people. Children diagnosed with AS/HFA often enjoy board games as they contain orderly systems and rules these children like to follow. The following section outlines the various ways board games can be used to build connection between parents and children diagnosed with AS/HFA.

TOGETHERNESS

Board games contain the constant theme of "togetherness." One cannot play a board game alone; the purpose is on the box: Two to Four Players. I wrote earlier how many children diagnosed with AS/HFA are sometimes baffled by activities that involve others. These children tend to be very comfortable playing alone and thus they seek out games and activities that are solitary in nature. I have found when a parent invites the child to join in a board game, the child usually responds in a positive way and like a detective wants to investigate the characteristics of the particular game. Many parents make the mistake of *assuming* the child is not going to want to play the game and thus never ask; parents of children diagnosed with AS/HFA must remember to make the invitation. Parents of children diagnosed with AS/HFA must also turn off the switch inside them that looks for the child to react like a neurotypical child when a game is introduced. The parent cannot go by the outward reaction of the child; instead, the parent must press on and continue with purposeful and intentional invitations to the child to join them in playing the board game. By making themselves available, the parent continually sends the message to the child that the child is valuable, and the parent desires time with him or her.

Social Skills Training

Along with the theme of "togetherness," board games offer parents the opportunity to model social skills. There are "social rules" found within a board game: Taking turns, listening, speaking in an articulate manner, and dealing with both frustration and exultation in appropriate ways can all be taught through playing a board game. This fact is important for children diagnosed with AS/HFA because they tend to see social situations as confusing, frightening, and annoying. Parents play an important role in teaching their children social skills, and playing a board game together provides a wonderful teaching platform and an opportunity for the parent to model the social skills I mentioned earlier. I use board games to show a child diagnosed with AS/HFA how social situations follow a sequence and a pattern. One person rolls a dice and moves his piece, and then the next person takes her turn. Sometimes during a person's turn there are extra "steps" (i.e. picking up a Chance card in Monopoly; deciding whether or not to take a shortcut, etc.). These sequences require a certain level of understanding and patience, just like in social situations. I like to map out to the young person and show him that social conversations and interactions are very much the same. One person speaks, and others listen. If the topic is something the person is knowledgeable about and wishes to comment on, she has the opportunity to do so. This helps to "demystify" the social "game" for the young person and also gives him a sense of confidence.

Modeling of Emotions within Relationship

Board games have a powerful modeling component that allows the parent/ caregiver the opportunity to demonstrate various emotional states as well as important communication strategies while playing the game. One of the common themes I encounter with the children with whom I work is they hate to lose. Accepting losing is an important part of life as there is a great deal more losing situations than winning ones and through game play children can become aware of this and accept it which helps them build resilience when disappointments come later in life. I never "let" children win when I play with them because they can usually tell when I am not playing my best, and then when they do win, the victory is that much sweeter for the child. When I lose I make sure I show I am disappointed, but I also make sure I express congratulations to the winner and also praise them on a job well done. This exchange shows I am fully aware of "losing" and losing does not feel good, but I also show excitement and praise for the child who won. In this way, I am modeling how to deal with disappointment and how to express it, as well as modeling encouragement and praise for another person. These interactions played out over time begin to make a lasting impression on the child diagnosed with AS/HFA.

GENERAL LEARNING

Board games also provide opportunities for general learning and allow the parent to be in a teaching role when parents play a board game with their child diagnosed with AS/HFA. I tell parents often that they represent the greatest teacher their child will ever have. I encourage them to not give that away to a school system or assume the parent has nothing to offer. What a tragedy! Instead, I encourage them to seek out every opportunity to be a teacher in every situation. I firmly believe that every person is a genius in their own way, regardless of their level of formal education, and all people bring a vast knowledge with them wherever they go. I try to get parents to see their children want to be taught; the child yearns to know what dad knows and what mom knows. Playing board games with your child allows this to happen! You get to teach about math, strategy, decision making, as well as everyday things like how things are made, how things work, and the ingredients of various career paths.

Imaginary Games

Children diagnosed with AS/HFA do not typically engage in imaginative play; however, I have come across many who do. I have decided to include a section on this because I encounter parents from time to time that tell me their child has created a world in which the child immerses himself in and the parents are witnesses to this amazing phenomenon. If you are one of these parents/caregivers, I think you are very blessed and I want to give you some ideas for using this phenomenon as a way to build connection with your child. First, remember you can set limits with your involvement in the play with your child as I mentioned earlier. You can set a timer to let your child know that when the timer goes off, you have to go back to what you were doing before you made yourself available to play with your child. This helps set boundaries which are important for the child to learn and also conserves your emotional and physical energy. The intensity of the child diagnosed with AS/HFA is remarkable and you are no match for this intensity! By setting limits you provide yourself with insulation so you are able to stay engaged with the child instead of becoming fatigued and going into "shutdown" mode.

A second thing to remember is to simply make yourself available to your child and ask him what role he would like for you to take in the imaginary world. I encourage parents to let their guards down and be free to be a villain, a co-conspirator, a hero with amazing powers, and so on. One of the valuable parts of my work is I allow myself to join imaginary play with children and be a part of their world through acting out whatever role they want me to have. Because I do this on a regular basis I find it fairly easy to do, but I have to consciously shed my adult "armor" and allow myself to be free to play. I often find that parents have difficulty "shifting gears" out of "adult mode" to enter play. However, I encourage them to go slowly and pretend that they are actors signing up to be in a play and that there is a director who is going to tell them exactly what to do. I help the parent see the benefits of doing this are many!

Benefits from Imaginary Play: Modeling and Building of Trust

First, the child gets to see the parent become multi-dimensional in their personalities and roles. We forget that our children tend to see us only "one way" most of the time; that is, "adult-manager-get-r-done" mode where we are tackling problems, buying groceries, and being taxi drivers. Remember when I told you that parents play an important role in the socialization behavior of their children diagnosed with AS/HFA? Well, this is part of that process. Children diagnosed with AS/HFA also tend to be "one dimensional" as well, but by watching their parent/caregiver be multi-dimensional in personality and roles, this makes a strong impact on their perspective of others and the world around them. So, when a dad who is usually "all business," gets down on the floor and grabs a LEGO® Bionicle figure and joins his child in fighting off the evil intruders, there is not only a deeper connection created between them but the child sees dad in a new way, which leads to the child seeing that it is "ok" for play, silliness, and seriousness to be part of a person.

A second powerful component of parents and caregivers joining in pretend, imaginary play with their child is the building of trust. I often emphasize the idea of trust and the important role trust plays with parents and I share with them that trust is something that is not fixed and does not stay in one developmental place. When a couple gets married, there is a level of trust, but through experiences and circumstances that trust can either go to new levels which are stronger and deeper or it can stay where it is and usually will be broken by the pressure that comes with new and challenging circumstances such as bills, children, and work. The same is true for the parent/child relationship. When the parent meets the needs of the child when the child is small, there is a level of trust that is built. The child is able to say "Mom will feed me, clothe me, and get me to school. Therefore I trust her." As the children develop however, their emotional, physical, and mental needs grow, and their awareness of the world around them increases. With this growth, the child needs more from the parent and is more aware of how trustworthy the parent is. If the parent does not recognize this and continues to meet the child's needs only on the base levels and does not grow and adapt to the child's changing needs, the child will sense this and by the time the child reaches the adolescent years, the adolescent will not trust the parent has the adolescent's best interest in mind.

Many parents react to this phenomenon by becoming more controlling and suspicious of their child who is now an adolescent. This explains why, when children naturally want more freedom to explore the world and be free to express who they are, the parent feels threatened and tightens their grip on the child. Instead of teaching valuable skills the adolescent needs for life the parent becomes the "warden" and out of their own fear the parent responds by clamping down, operating in a fear-based manner. While this works for a while in keeping the adolescent "safe" and "out of trouble" (and sadly, this reinforces the parent's idea that what he or she is doing is "right") the relationship between the parent and the adolescent is damaged because the adolescent no longer believes the parent has the adolescent's best interest in mind. A great way for a parent to make this shift in meeting their child's mental and emotional needs as the child grows into new developmental stages is to engage in imaginative play with him or her on a regular basis.

For the parent with a child diagnosed with AS/HFA, the building of trust is a significant component in the relationship between child and parent. Children diagnosed with AS/HFA often have difficulty in social situations and relationships and it can be easy for them to not trust others. This is not because the child is antisocial, but because relationships and social interactions tend to be confusing for the child, and it is natural to be afraid of and want to avoid that which we do not understand. Thus, the child usually forms a bond with few individuals, and the parents/caregivers tend to be the main ones. Many of the children I work with are intensely bonded to their mothers; some however, are more bonded to their father. Sometimes this creates problems for the parents because the child sees the parent as a security blanket and is afraid to go anywhere or do anything without the parent present. This dependence puts a great strain on the relationship between child and parent. Like I wrote earlier, the bond of trust was formed but as the child diagnosed with AS/HFA is moving into new developmental stages, they have become less trustful and more dependent, instead of more trusting and independent. Many of you may find yourself in this very predicament as you are reading this, and I have sat with many frustrated parents who tells me they are about to reach their breaking point.

I help these parents see that one of the best ways to help with building trust in new developmental stages with their children is to engage in imaginary play with the child. This is very beneficial for the child diagnosed with AS/HFA because it helps the child see the parent in a multi-dimensional way and through play the parent can take on other roles (i.e. villain, hero, ally, etc.). This helps establish trust in two ways. First, the child sees the parent can and does have other roles to play in life such as bill payer, worker, and caretaker of other family members such as grandparents, siblings, etc. This helps pull children diagnosed with AS/HFA out of "tunnel-vision" mode and forces them to see things from another perspective. Children diagnosed with AS/HFA can be very one-dimensional in their thinking and can have difficulty seeing things from another perspective. This also plays a role in explaining why these children struggle with trusting only a select few: They tend to put their "eggs" into one or two baskets. Through play, the child can see that mom or dad has to spend time with other people and do other things. This helps when the parent must pull away from the child and also helps push the child into being less dependent on mom or dad.

A second reason that imaginary play helps establish trust is in allowing parents to connect themes that relate to real life into their relationship with the child. I worked with a dad who was very fearful about his son becoming so dependent on his parents that he would not be able to be independent in the future. I challenged this father to connect with his son through play and to use this as a vehicle of teaching his son about independence. His son loved to play out scenes from movies and video games. The father adopted several character roles from these movies and games and found a way to incorporate teaching themes of independence, being self-reliant, and "thinking on your own two feet" into the play sessions with his son. He was able to channel connection from fear and turned the fear into something productive, instead of something destructive. For instance, one scenario the boy created had he and his father working together to defeat a bad guy. Part of the time the father played the role to a tee, standing by his son and helping him, but then he changed the course of the play and told his son that he had to stand on his own and fight and the father was going to tend to something else for a while. Sure enough, the father re-emerged after a few minutes and the bad guy was defeated. After the play, the father and son reviewed what happened, and the father told his son that he did that because one day the son will be living on his own without mom and dad there all of the time. This began a mental shift for the boy and was instrumental in helping paint a picture in his mind of living on his own someday. This was a perfect example of play therapy done by a parent and how powerful a teaching tool it can be!

Electronics: Video/Computer Games

One of the topics I discuss with parents almost every week relates to video games. Parents are either concerned these games are going to "rot my kid's brain" or "turn him into a serial killer." I used video and computer games in my dissertation work and found them to be very useful. I play video games myself and grew up with the "Nintendo Generation;" I witnessed how the games that were once only reserved for the arcade became accessible to be played in the privacy of one's home. Because I meet with children and adolescents daily, I am keenly aware the role these games play for young people in providing them not only fun, but also an identity and a sense of belonging to something. I want to help you as a parent see a different side to these games and also provide you with a "toolbox" in using electronic games as a way to connect with your child in a new and fun way.

BENEFITS OF ELECTRONIC GAME PLAY

Creating/Interacting in Their Own World. There are several benefits of electronic game play. First, computer and video games provide an opportunity for the child to create the child's own personal "world," allowing him to interact through the game and play out various social and "real-world" situations. Children diagnosed with AS/HFA are usually drawn to solitary activities, but I am passionate about helping parents see this can be a path towards greater connection with their child and that computer/video games do contain themes the parent can use to teach social skills. One boy I worked with loved to play the game RuneScape, a game that involved guiding a figure through a medieval world and completing various tasks in order to garner possessions, food, and money. This game is a known as a multiplayer online role-playing game (MORPG) and this young man was "obsessed," according to his mother. When I asked her if she knew anything about it, she said "No, I'm not into video games." This is a common response that I get from parents regarding video/ computer games, and I often respond that the parent probably was not that much into Barney or potty training, but we all did what we had to do. While this may sound sarcastic, I am passionate about getting the parent to see we must be flexible and become involved in what our children love, instead of shunning them because what they love "is not what I am into."

I was able to help this boy's mother see the vast world of RuneScape and that the game contained real world themes of work, interaction, danger, protection, and preparation. The game also models social interaction and one must communicate with others in the game in order to advance. Once this perspective was provided, she was able to change how she approached her son's "obsession." Instead of seeing the game playing as a "frivolous" activity, she was able to see how important it was for her son to have this private, safe world. This also helped her learn how her son approached and solved problems, and gave her a new appreciation of how hard he was willing to work to accomplish goals. I suggested that she sit with him and watch him play. She looked at me as if I had asked her to play with a snake. "What for?" she asked. "To get in his world," I replied. "To let him see through your action you are telling him he matters and that what he loves is something you want to find out about." "Oh, he doesn't care," she replied curtly. "He doesn't even notice…he does his thing and I do my thing." "Do it and see what happens," I suggested. She did and reaped the rewards of connecting with her son and learning more about him than she ever thought possible. She even began playing the game with him.

This mother's attitude reflects many parents' perceptions that children diagnosed with AS/HFA do not need social interaction; that the child can be left alone because the child does not respond to affection and does not interact the way neurotypical children do and this means the parent does not need to interact with them. Not so! I wrote earlier how these individuals diagnosed with AS/HFA desire connection with others and how important the modeling of relationship is for these individuals, especially when they are children. Even though the child may not like giving and receiving affection, the parent/caregiver must not give up or make false assumptions. Children diagnosed with AS/HFA find activities that help them feel safe, and often the safest world they know is getting lost in a video/computer game. If parents are willing to expand their minds and branch out and learn something new, the world of video/computer games represents a great way to build connection and relationship.

Problem Solving. A second benefit of electronic game play is for the child to practice solving problems. Video/computer games always have themes of challenges, failure, practice, and reaching new levels. Each level of a game has new challenges and requires increased skill. I find this to be a wonderful metaphor for life. I like to use video/computer games with children struggling with all sorts of problems from impulse control to low self-worth. I use the games to show that life happens in small stages and scenes, each section of the day is a collections of frames put together just like in a video game. For example, when I work with a child struggling with impulse control issues, I use the games to show the child how she has the ability to create small "frames" and segments of time; and within that "frame" she has choices that she can make, just like in a video or computer game. One game that I like to use is Super Mario Bros. because many children recognize the figures of Mario, Luigi, and Bowser. I show them that within each section they have many choices: Go down a pipe, jump on a bad guy, try for a mushroom, and so on. Each move a player chooses creates other options, and so on. To successfully get through the level, children must stay out of danger and make good choices in addition to keeping their focus on the main goal: reaching the finish line. One of the joys of my work is when the child I am working with suddenly understands this concept because of the application that is made to life through a video game, and reaps the positive benefits of making good choices.

For parents, this concept is powerful because they are able to see their children's problem solving abilities and also teach problem solving strategies through video/computer game play. I will often have children play a game they have never played before, and from that experience I can tell a lot about how their mind works and how they approach problem solving. I can also use the experience to teach decision making and strategizing to help them not only be successful in the game, but also in life. I encourage parents to be researchers and observers of their children, to watch how they think, act, learn, and respond emotionally to various situations and people.

Electronic gaming is a wonderful way to do this. And not only is it another pathway to connecting with your child, it is a valuable tool to learn more about your child.

Experiencing Failure. Anyone who has attempted to play an electronic game in any form will be confronted immediately with a common phenomenon: Failure. Failure is a common theme in life, and games allow individuals to become acquainted with the experience of failure and to teach us that failure is survivable. This is an important concept for children to grasp and they can learn how to cope with failure through game play. Usually this experience and knowledge is then transferred to real life. I discussed earlier how play helps us practice "real life" stuff, and learning to experience failure and deal with it is definitely one of those valuable characteristics of play. Video/computer games have some unique features related to failure. First, failure reminds us it is through failing and "messing up" that we learn. When children (or anyone, for that matter) begin playing a video/computer game for the first time, they usually fail but then they learn from their mistakes and gradually become better at playing the game. The experience of failure can cause a great many emotional reactions; frustration, disappointment, and anger are common. Behavior reactions such as yelling, stomping, or withdrawal are also common. Psychological reactions such as negative thinking or negative mood may occur. There may also be physiological reactions such as increased heart rate, increased breathing, or a pounding headache. All of these are interconnected and can be triggered by the experience of failure.

Children in general tend to struggle with failure. They do not like it, and if we are honest, none of us do. Children diagnosed with AS/HFA often see things in black or white with one-dimensional thinking, and often struggle with failure. This struggle can be a factor for the child relating to others and being hesitant in joining in social activities with other children. One boy diagnosed with AS/HFA came to me for counseling and he struggled with failure. When he lost at something, he would have emotional "meltdowns;" throwing things, hitting himself, and crying. After the incident he would stay in an "upset" state for an hour or more. This led to many problems with the boy being able to join in activities with peers and forming friendships. By the time he came for counseling, he was virtually isolated from any social interaction and was unable to attend regular school. One of the first things I did with him was set him up to play a simple video game that he was very excited to play. He went along fairly well and then misjudged a jump and his character fell into a chasm and his turn was over. He screamed so loud I lifted off my seat and he threw the controller down on the floor. He then slid out of his chair and fell to the floor and began to cry. He cried in an inconsolable manner for almost twenty minutes. When he got himself somewhat under control, I attempted to get him to try the game again, but to no avail. At the next session, he did attempt the game and did better, but once again he experienced a meltdown when he could not complete a level. I began working with him on understanding what happened in his body that made him feel so out of control, and I was able to teach him emotional control techniques. For this boy, the slightest emotional irritation of frustration or sadness was nearly unbearable for him. School officials and other professionals labeled this behavior as "oppositional-defiant" and "needing a good spanking" but I saw this as one of the "quirks" that sometimes accompanies AS/HFA. While this was hard for me to observe, I was able to help this boy through sharing the experience with him and the video games proved very useful in helping him learn frustration tolerance. Each time we played he did better and better, and soon he was able to experience failure without reacting. My heart leaped with joy when the boy joined one of my social groups and was able to experience failure while playing a game and he did not react negatively or have a "meltdown." One of the great joys of my work is watching a child such as this as he gained valuable skills that will help him be successful by both controlling his emotions and in his ability to connect with others. Through the simple act of playing a video game, this boy was able to learn valuable skills that changed his life.

A Social Experience. Another benefit of electronic game play is it can be a valuable social experience. Many of the video/computer/handheld device games are able to be connected to a network that allows the player to connect with other players from within their own home to all over the world. One young man told me in my office, "If it weren't for the ability to connect with other people through playing my game, I wouldn't have ever learned to talk with other people. It made it easier when I had to get out in the real world." Like many individuals diagnosed with AS/HFA, he shied away from contact with people following severe bullying in middle school that resulted in him being home-schooled. He began playing a popular computer game that connected him with people on the internet, and soon found that since he did not have to make eye contact, it was easier for him to communicate through text and voice. He actually formed deep connections with his gaming "friends" and he helped me see what a strong sense of community that exists in the gaming world and that he and his friends connected about much more than just the game. For instance, he showed me how one of the members' mother was in the hospital and I could see the many messages of hope and encouragement sent to this hurting friend; I could also see that the messages and discussions were about politics, careers, fears, funny jokes and stories, and just life in general. The game brought them together, but the bonds formed were related to the similar struggles that every human being faces.

Video game consoles such as the PlayStation 3, Xbox360, and the Nintendo Wii provide opportunities for social connection through playing games. There are a myriad of games that have two player options and provide wonderful opportunities for connection between parents and children. The most common complaint I hear from parents is that they do not know how to play video games and my response is always the same: "No one knows how to play when they are first introduced to a game, but we all can learn." I remind parents of the fact that when the focus is on building connection with their child, the thought of the parent's ability to play the game or worrying about looking foolish goes out the window. My dissertation work provided me with an up-close view of how powerful two-player games can be. One of the types of games I used was LEGO® Star Wars and LEGO® Indiana Jones. These games have a unique two-player option that allows two players to work together while completing the level. While one player is fighting off the bad guys, the other player can gather important artifacts and turn levers, or both can join in fighting enemies. The players work as one unit, communicating and sharing the duties of the game. I discovered that this was very powerful, especially for the young people I worked with who were diagnosed with AS/HFA and who struggled with relating to others.

One surprising thing I discovered in playing these games with young people was a bond of trust and connection formed between the child and me. By working together to solve the level we were playing, the child and I had to communicate and rely on each other's abilities. This process was remarkable and I discovered this would be a great way for parents to build relationship with their children on many levels. Trust is one of the most important elements of any relationship, but it is especially important for parents and children, and especially parents of children diagnosed with AS/HFA. As I have written earlier, children diagnosed with AS/HFA often struggle with trusting others and are often hyper-vigilant (being extra-extra careful) in testing for safety with people and their surroundings. Through playing a two-player game, the relationship between the child and parent goes to a new level of experience, and in doing so a greater foundation of trust is built.

This experience also allows the parent to be seen in a different light and display different characteristics that the child may not usually see. The parent can laugh, show excitement, and also be able to encourage the child through the experience of playing the game. As I have written earlier, this is very important because the parent is an important influence on the child's emotional and social development. Any time we as parents can pull ourselves out of "manager" mode and show a lighter, more fun, and human side, the better it is for relationship building with our children. When a parent models frustration or sorrow over "failing" a level in a video game it is powerful for the child diagnosed with AS to see. Conversely, modeling characteristics such as optimism and emotional control through problem solving and working together is also powerful. As the parent and child work together through video or computer game play the foundation is laid for greater trust, social learning, and deeper connection.

BUILDING CONNECTION THROUGH ELECTRONIC GAME PLAY

One great area that I see this work wonderfully is with the dynamic of a single mom with a child diagnosed with AS/HFA who is really into tech toys and games. Moms usually feel lost when it comes to games and toys that are technologically advanced, not because they are not smart enough to master them, but because they usually have not spent a lot of time around "gadgets." Many of the mothers I come in contact with usually share their feelings of being "shut out" when it comes to connecting with their child diagnosed with AS/HFA simply because they did not play with "techie" toys/games when they were young and moms are usually so busy with the day-to-day child rearing duties (i.e. feeding, clothing, preparing, etc.), that they do not allow themselves time to immerse themselves into play. I really get excited when I encounter these moms because I take their passion for connection and simply shed light on the path to make it happen. However, I have to teach them a few simple steps in order to get things going:

1. Show genuine interest. No faking or you will be found out!
2. Adopt a teachable spirit. "Just Be" and stay in the moment!
3. Don't ask too many questions. This is annoying!
4. Remember that this is an opportunity to show a "fun" side of you!
5. Fight discouragement! No one is skilled the first time they play a video/ computer game!

Most of the children I work with seem disappointed their parent does not at least make an attempt to play video games with them. And most of the parents I talk to carry the belief their child does not want them to join them in the play or at least sit and watch them. When parents do try to join in a game with their child, I find the parents get discouraged and quickly give up, never to try again. I remind parents that they must continue to try and give their best, and to fight discouragement.

I recommend two player games for parents to play with their child as these allow for the parent to join their child in the action. All of the LEGO® games all have really great two player formats and create a sense of the two players helping each other and conquering together (i.e. LEGO® Indiana Jones, LEGO® Star Wars, LEGO® Harry Potter, and so on). The Nintendo Wii offers several games that can be done together, as do the other gaming consoles. The main thing to remember is that the purpose of joining in electronic game play is to build connection and for your child to see you in a different way that provides new avenues for trust and social learning to take place. Let down your guard and focus on connection and just "be" in the moment with your child; it is a magical and wondrous place and your only task is to simply be curious about what you will find there.

CHAPTER 5

*Relationship Barriers and Parent Qualities Necessary in Building Connection
with Adolescents Diagnosed with AS/HFA*

I discussed in Chapter Three some of the barriers that exist in building relationship
with children diagnosed with AS/HFA and many of the same barriers exist when
it comes to building relationship with adolescents. I decided to write this section
a bit differently. I have written this chapter as a way to help parents understand
what occurs during development in the adolescent years in the physical, mental, and
emotional categories and then I have applied that information to make it relevant
to adolescents diagnosed with AS/HFA. I have done this because I believe it is
important for parents raising adolescents diagnosed with AS/HFA to have a solid
understanding of how the brain, body, and emotional components are changing and
interacting as the young person moves toward development. I believe this foundation of knowledge helps the parent in being able to better understand the adolescent
diagnosed with AS/HFA and also have a picture of where the young person is in his
or her development and what is going on inside the adolescent. It is easy for parents
of adolescents diagnosed with AS/HFA to forget that beneath the challenges that
they are dealing with are the normal developmental changes and hormonal upheaval
that goes on in all adolescents, regardless of the presence of AS/HFA or not.

Physical Development during Adolescence

Obviously, adolescence is a time of intense physical change. These physical changes
are the visible effects of chemical changes going on inside the body. Rapid bone
growth that results in the lengthening of limbs is one of the most visible signs
during this stage. For girls, the body begins to take shape and the menstrual cycle
begins. Adolescent boys often appear clumsy and act as though they do not know
what to do with their longer limbs. Many adolescents experience physical pain
because of the intense growth, as the rapidly growing bones and ligaments stretch

while the rest of the body races to catch up. Acne, facial and pubic hair, and voice change are a few other physical changes that happen seemingly overnight. Sexual changes occur and can often leave the adolescent with yet another layer of wonder and insecurity creating feelings of uneasiness and doubt yet excitement at the thought of becoming an adult. Underneath the surface is a surge of chemicals that are released into the body that propels the young person ever onward towards adulthood. While these changes often seem to happen overnight to the parent and others who come in contact with the young person, we must remember that the young person often feels the same way. I have had adolescents tell me that they feel afraid of the changes in their body and one said, "I feel like I don't know what to do with myself" when talking about how he had grown four inches in just a few months.

From a physical standpoint alone, adolescence is a time when young people are feeling awkward and unsure of their new stature and body form. I try to get parents to revisit their adolescence and remember their own feelings of awkwardness, and I encourage them to talk about what they remember about the changes in their physical body. I think this is important because it helps put the parents in the shoes of their adolescent in at least a small way. I find parents often dismiss me as I try to help them see that the road of the adolescent of today is much more complicated and challenging than it was "in their day"; many do not want to accept this way of thinking but I remind them that their parents were disconnected from their struggles as well. Parents of today assume that with all of the technological advances of modern times that adolescents have a sort of paradise; yet I find adolescents are even more confused and lost as a result of all the technological advances of today. I am a firm believer we as parents must tap into our memories of awkwardness and feelings of self-doubt during our adolescence as a way to build connection with our children as they move through this challenging yet miraculous time.

Physical Changes and the Adolescent Diagnosed with AS/HFA

While there are a great many challenges to any adolescent going through the many physical changes that occur during puberty, physical changes are even more difficult for adolescents diagnosed with AS/HFA. I wrote earlier how children and adolescents diagnosed with AS/HFA often have difficulty with coordination of body movements and many seem to be disconnected from their bodies. When puberty hits, these young people tend to experience even more confusion that comes with longer limbs and other changes related to the march towards adulthood. In addition to this, that these young people already feel rejected by peer groups and often believe that they do not "fit" with the "normal" kids; the physical explosion of puberty only magnifies the confusion that adolescents diagnosed with AS/HFA tend to experience. Many people falsely believe these adolescents do not struggle because these young people tend to not say much about their difficulties; however, we must remember this does not mean that these amazing young people do not suffer.

I have sat with many adolescents that struggle with the challenges that AS/HFA who share with me the embarrassment they feel about the rapid changes in their bodies. Many of the young people I work with hate P.E. and physical activities because much peer rejection and bullying surrounds these activities due to being uncoordinated, and the onset of puberty amplifies this hatred of anything that involves physical movement. I often help parents understand this phenomenon and tell them all of us tend to avoid activities that were the source of rejection and ridicule from our peers. Many of these young people have been made fun of since pre-school, where they first discovered that kicking, catching a ball, and running were not activities they enjoyed. Girls diagnosed with AS/HFA are often confused with the new shape that their bodies begin to take and are "horrified" that they will now be more noticed, despite their best efforts to stay "unnoticed." Obviously, more acne, body odor, and clumsiness only add to the sometimes daily ritual of being rejected and ridiculed. I will discuss bullying in later sections and also help parents find ways to deal with it, but bullying is an ongoing problem for those who appear and act differently, especially in the middle school years.

What can parents do to help their adolescent diagnosed with AS/HFA deal with the physical changes in their bodies? First, communicate to the young person how his body is changing and help him understand what is happening and what is going to happen. Use this information as a way to reassure her and help connect her to her body. I find many young people diagnosed with AS/HFA are disconnected from their bodies because they are uncoordinated and tend to see their body as a "thing" and not part of bigger system: themselves. I believe that parents play a large role in guiding their young person through the rough waters of puberty, and especially when the young person already struggles with the challenges that AS/HFA brings. A second helpful role for parents is sharing their own struggles and communicating to the young person he or she is not alone. I find the parents are the people the adolescent trusts the most, and when parents share their stories it can do a great deal to empower the young person. Third, the parent can join and bond with the young person in new ways to provide a sense of security and stability during the time of puberty. I will discuss techniques to build this connection in Chapter Six.

Sexual Development and Adolescence

Sexual development also occurs during adolescence and is responsible for many of the physical and emotional changes that I discussed in the earlier sections. I remind parents who are experiencing a difficult time dealing with the emotional and behavioral explosions of their adolescent that this period of time is much like a volcano erupting: It happens fast; is unpredictable; it is hard to see what is going on beneath the surface; and it is a very messy process. On a more positive note, however, it is a miraculous process at the same time. I feel it is important to discuss the sexual development of the adolescent to review what is going on in the body and how this affects the young person emotionally and cognitively and then I will explain what this means for the adolescent diagnosed with AS/HFA.

Hormones

Hormones play an integral role in creating the many changes that occur during adolescence. Hormones gradually build up in a child's body beginning around age eight, and by ten or eleven those hormones are getting ready to be released. The pituitary gland releases large quantities of hormones that results in the development of sperm in the testicles of the male and the development of the eggs in the ovaries of the female, as well as other secondary sexual characteristics. The intense release of hormones continues over a period of a few years and gradually the young person begins to appear more adult-like. This hormonal "explosion" is important not only for sexual development, but also lays the groundwork for the development of the nervous system, which is important for performing greater responsibilities such as adult decision making and emotional control.

Hormones and the Nervous System

Researchers have long known that the period of adolescence is crucial for the development of the adult nervous system which leads towards better decision making, learning social skills, and control of emotions that are necessary to be successful in the adult world. Recent studies have shown that the timing of the release of hormones is important for development of "neural pathways," which are the series of circuits in the nervous system that allow the growth of mature thinking and behavior.[13] The reason I believe it is important for parents to know about this is because it helps explain why one day an adolescent can seem as mature as a thirty year old, and then the next day have a tantrum like a child over a seemingly insignificant event. It also helps explain why adolescents can make very unwise decisions, even when they are likely to get caught or hurt themselves. Parents often remark to me after their adolescent has been arrested or suspended from school; "How could he/she have done something so stupid? It's as if they didn't have a brain at all!" I explain the process of brain development in adolescents and tell the parent that there are times when the logic and reasoning sequences are not engaged. During adolescence the brain is in a state of development that is not always even and neatly organized, and very often the development of the new circuitry resembles a "two steps forward and one step back" process.

One picture I use to get people to think about this concept is to picture a tract of land that is currently full of scrub brush and rocks and is going to be turned into a housing development complete with beautiful homes, roads, and fountains. When one looks at the picture of the proposal that the developer has painted, and then at the land that is raw and unformed, it is hard to believe the final product will ever be a reality. Then the trucks, tractors, and land movers come in and begin shaping the land. Scrub brush and old trees are removed, and rocks and unwanted materials are gathered, piled high, and hauled away. Smoothers arrive and begin shaping the land and creating what will soon be lots for homes and roads connecting the sections together. Even at this point, with everything stripped bare, it can be even harder to believe the land is going to come close to looking like what the developer has proposed. Piles of dirt and rock are shifted, but no form seems to be taking shape; and sometimes the big piles sit and seem to mock the workers who are trying to shape the land. But then, something happens. Almost overnight, roads are paved, lots are bought, and foundations begin are laid. Trees and bushes are planted and gates and

---

[13] Sisk, Cheryl L, and Julia L Zehr. 2005. "Pubertal hormones organize the adolescent brain and behavior." *Frontiers In Neuroendocrinology* 26, no. 3-4: 163-174.

walls are put in place. Gradually, the land begins to take shape, until finally, it is orderly and beautiful, fully functional and ready for homes to be built and for families to move into them.

This picture helps demonstrate how brain development happens. There is an order and development that keeps moving forward, but sometimes it is slow and without visible outward signs of progress. This helps explain the "back and forth" process of maturity and development that often is so frustrating to parents. Add to this frustration, as the adolescent is often confused by these shifts and changes and is bombarded by the emotions of fear and frustration which can come out as anger. This is why I stress the importance of parents and caregivers being non-reactive and controlling their emotional responses because an emotional response will only create further problems. If the parent and the adolescent go into "fight-or-flight" mode, damaging words are spoken and long lasting emotional wounds are inflicted. The opportunity to teach the adolescent by using firm boundaries is lost; the opportunity for the parent to model unconditional love through connection is missed. When young people "freak out" emotionally, they often crave an adult presence to provide boundaries and a presence of strength and love. If the parent reacts, it can send the message to the young person that "Mom or Dad is not strong enough to help me; I'm not sure I can trust them." Please know I am not advocating for a parent who is being screamed at by an angry adolescent to just sit and take it; the parent may need to raise their voice or adopt a forceful presence to get the young person's attention and remind the young person that he needs to get control of his emotions. However, I do know that a firm, calm voice, and a non-reactive presence will usually de-escalate an angry, emotional person. I will address parenting issues in Chapter Seven.

Hormones and Emotional Reactivity: Mood Swings and Stress

The release of hormones during adolescence creates a flood of physical, mental, and emotional reactions in the body. Hormone levels become imbalanced and this creates a chain of various reactions in which adolescents are flooded by thoughts, feelings, and sensations that they cannot understand or control. The overall result is stress: Stress from their ability to put feelings into words, stress in understanding what is going on in their bodies, and stress from feeling as though the demands of life outweigh the resources to cope. Recent research shows one of the hormones that is released in the brain that helps adults deal with stress successfully actually causes anxiety during puberty for the adolescent.[14] This means that during the time of increased brain development in adolescence, the very hormones that will eventually keep the brain calm in adulthood work against the young person and create tension and a sense of anxiety. For the adolescent, this means there is heightened anxiety without the coping skills to manage it. Because the adolescent does not have the ability to manage the anxiety, they often resort to yelling, tantrums, or blindly blaming others for their problems. (*Parent:* "Could you explain why you failed your history test after you told me that you studied for it?" *Adolescent:* "My teacher is a jerk and hates me and my friends.")

When I work with people and the topic of stress comes up there is a phrase that I share with them: "Stress-regress." What this means is that when people are under stress, they will often regress or go back to a more childish or immature way of dealing with the situation. For example, some people will become stressed by waiting for something that, in their opinion, is taking too long. It might be standing in line at the grocery store or waiting for food at a restaurant. You will often hear comments and see behavior that is quite childish, such as yelling or stomping about. Even though the person is an adult, and even though the context of the situation is not threatening at all, people often deal with stress through regressive behavior and attitudes. This is a common phenomenon for adolescents and I think that it is helpful for parents/caregivers to remember this little phrase: "Stress-Regress." When your adolescent is "freaking out" emotionally over a seemingly insignificant problem, do not demean them or dismiss their feelings. They are really feeling stress; their brain is in "fight-or-flight"; they are overwhelmed and confused. The adolescent is "freaking out" because the stress they are experiencing leaves them with the coping skills of a two year old. Do you think it would really help to make fun of them in that moment or tell them what they are worried about is stupid and insignificant? Instead, connect with them in a calm and relaxed manner, listen to them with the purpose of understanding, and hand the problem back to them with open-ended questions such as "What can you do about that?" or "What are some solutions you can think of?" which helps to remove the pressure off the parent and helps focus on the relationship between parent and adolescent. I will talk about this in the next chapter when I discuss building closer connection and relationship with adolescents.

---

[14] Adolescent Mood Swings. *ScienceDaily.* Retrieved January 26, 2012,
     from http://www.sciencedaily.com /releases/2007/03/070311202019.htm

Sexual Development and the Adolescent Diagnosed with AS/HFA

The onset of puberty and the sexual development of adolescence can be a confusing and lonely time for the young person diagnosed with AS/HFA. As I have already explained, individuals diagnosed with AS/HFA tend to be confused by emotions, and the journey of adolescence can be an emotional blizzard. I have worked with many adolescents diagnosed with AS/HFA who have shared with me feelings of sadness, anger, fear, and frustration over being rejected, not understanding who they are, feeling like they do not fit in, and wondering if they are damaged because they had not experienced a sexual interest in boys or girls yet. From the earlier sections, you can see how difficult navigating the waters of AS/HFA can be for these young people in general, but add to this the challenges of sexual development and it can be a whole different challenge indeed. I must remind the reader that individuals diagnosed with AS/HFA experience the same sexual desires, interests, and changes as neurotypical individuals, but they have a hard time processing emotions and communicating those thoughts and feelings to others.[15] This underscores the importance of the young person having parents and caregivers who are willing to work to build a strong bond with the adolescent; parents and caregivers willing to become people that the individual diagnosed with AS/HFA can go to, rely on, and who can develop an understanding of the difficulties that the young person is having.

Parents in American culture have long struggled with being able to talk to their young people about sex related matters. Adolescents are often left to fend for themselves because parents are either militant about the topic or completely silent, leaving young people to learn what they can through pornography, a friend's experiences, and their own experimentation. Perhaps nowhere else in the world exists such double standard: sex is still taboo yet the use of sex to sell products is jammed in our faces from the time we can walk. Parents/caregivers of adolescents diagnosed with AS/HFA face these same feelings and other obstacles when thinking about talking with their young person about sex. Many parents of adolescents diagnosed with AS/HFA incorrectly assume that they do not need to talk about sexual development or anything related to sex; parents assume that because of the barriers in expressing

---

[15] Hénault, Isabelle. 2006. *Asperger's syndrome and sexuality: From adolescence through adulthood.* London England: Jessica Kingsley Publishers, 2006.

emotions and thoughts the young person will never need to know about this topic. These parents could not be more wrong.

The truth is, adolescents diagnosed with AS/HFA need a parent who can help them put words to the feelings and thoughts they are experiencing and guide them through the myriad of situations and experiences adolescence brings. Parents need to be comfortable acting in the role of sexual educator and advocate, throwing aside feelings of being uncomfortable or embarrassed.[16] Because young people diagnosed with AS/HFA have difficulty expressing thoughts and emotions, sometimes they can feel sexual urges in a more intense manner and because of the lack of understanding of social boundaries these young people may act out these urges in inappropriate ways. Adolescence can also bring more intense rejection and bullying which also results in emotional overload for the young person. Many young people diagnosed with AS/HFA take feelings that they do not understand and create false attributions, which means the young person assumes something is wrong with *them* and that *they* have a problem and *deserve* the rejection they are experiencing. This false attribution is all the more reason to have parents that are able to guide, be an advocate, and educate their young people about boundaries, social skills, and what is going on inside their bodies.

The Problem of Communication

One of the main issues regarding discussing sexual issues is that adolescents, whether neurotypical or diagnosed with AS/HFA, often have a hard time dialoguing with parents and caregivers about such matters. As a counselor who works with young people on a daily basis I instruct parents to being discussing sexual development and sexual matters while the young person is still a child, so that the platform for discussing such matters is open. This way, young people are more comfortable and used to talking openly with their parents about these topics. One young man of fourteen who was diagnosed with AS/HFA was referred to me because he was saying sexually inappropriate things to girls at school. He had also gotten caught looking at pornography, for which he was severely punished. Like many young

---

[16] Attwood S, Powell J. *Making Sense Of Sex: A Forthright Guide To Puberty, Sex And Relationships For People With Asperger's Syndrome* [e-book]. London England: Jessica Kingsley Publishers; 2008.

people with whom I work, he was emotionally immature. This young man was being raised by his grandparents, who had very little experience talking with an adolescent about sexual matters. I built a relationship with him and we started to discuss what happened at school. When I asked the young man about what he said to the girls at school and looking at pornography, his head dropped and he remained silent for almost five straight minutes. He never looked at me again for the rest of the session.

Over the next few sessions I attempted to bring up the subject again and each time the young man would hang his head and fall silent. Once this happens I never push things; I fall silent also and gently remind the young person that when he is ready he can speak. I remind him or her that the counseling office is a safe place; I remind him or her that I will not judge or condemn. I decided to change my app-roach with this young man. Instead of bringing up the incidents, I began working on various emotions and the thoughts that were attached to them. He was a lover of Zelda the video game so we played the game while we talked about emotions such as anger, frustration, and fear. I use video games not only because it lowers the defenses of young people, but because there are themes contained in the games such as over-coming challenges, sequential thinking, and facing obstacles that require relying on others for help. He shared with me he was being picked on in school, not by boys but by girls. This young man was very socially awkward and was by nature very shy; some of the girls at his school thought it would be funny if they openly flirted with him and pretended to be interested in him. This caused a swirl of emotions in him from elation to fear to confusion. We talked about emotions and I explained what causes them and how what we think can elicit a series of emotions. Of course, he did not know what to do with this newfound attention by these girls or the feelings that ac-companied it. The girls would laugh when he gazed at them, dazed by the emotions and then he told me that other classmates would join in the laughter and he would get away as quickly as he could. This went on for weeks. The young man told no one about the encounters, and realized he was feeling a lot of emotion about the situa-tion; emotions he did not know what to do with. He told me that he felt angry; that these girls would pretend to like him and when they did not and were just playing with him. He was sad, because he noticed girls and liked them very much but he did not know how to talk to girls. He experienced frustration because their actions made him think that he would have friends and be liked, but then the so-called friends would laugh and leave him, like a mist that materialized and then quickly vanished.

The reason that I share this story is to show how hard it can be for young people diagnosed with AS/HFA to communicate their thoughts and feelings about something, especially when it is about a topic and they perceive is "bad" and also when they are "in trouble" for their behavior choices. None of us like to discuss things that embarrass us, and these young people are no different. This young man was confused by what he was feeling, and the more that I asked him about what he did the more emotionally shutdown he became. Instead, I chose a different path as I often do in order to foster communication with adolescents like this young man. Rather than waste time talking about what he did, I focused on the emotions and thoughts surrounding the events that he was experiencing. While what he did was wrong, we could not even begin to look at that until I was able to help him identify the thoughts and emotions that drove this behavior. This is very important for parents to understand when dealing with any adolescent, but especially for parents with adolescents diagnosed with AS/HFA. This is another reason why I stress to parents to control their reactivity because when they react, it is only damaging the relationship between themselves and their child and the natural weight of the situation is not felt because usually the adolescent becomes more worried about what the parent is feeling than finding insight into learning how to make better choices.

The Problem of Sexual Development Delays

Development does not happen in the same stages in the same manner for all young people during adolescence. Sometimes there are delays and not all of the "parts" come together fully at the same time. For instance, a girl may be late in developing physical characteristics such as breasts while a boy's voice may not change. While this is problematic for neurotypical young people as well as those diagnosed with AS/HFA, the latter may have a more difficult struggle because of the emotional and social difficulties that these young people encounter. For example, one young man that I worked with who was about seventeen was experiencing many negative feelings and was the target of bullying because of sexual development delays. For him, he still retained his childish appearance, his voice had not changed and he was worried because he knew that he was supposed to like girls but he did not feel "anything special" towards any of the girls that he knew. He also did not feel anything towards boys either; he made sure he wanted me to know. As you might expect, he was the target of ongoing bullying which caused further emotional and social problems for him.

I want to make it clear this does not mean this young man is "asexual," which is a term given to a small percentage of the population that have no sexual drive or interest in sex. A misconception exists which states many individuals diagnosed with AS/HFA are asexual because these individuals appear to not show an interest in romantic partners or sexual activity. However, there is no scientific data to support this idea. Because individuals diagnosed with AS/HFA encounter challenges in building and sustaining relationships they often avoid such relationships. I have encountered many young people diagnosed with AS/HFA who believe that if forming friendships and keep them are so much work, then the idea of finding a romantic partner must be utterly unattainable. They also share with me their thinking (based in logic, obviously) that the idea of putting up a false front in order to "win" a partner and then go through the seemingly arduous experience of dating seems completely ridiculous and a "waste of time." Thus, many young people diagnosed with AS/HFA sometimes go through a period of denial and completely reject the thought of seeking a partner, which tends to make them appear as though they are asexual when this is not really the case.

For this young man, his feelings of not being "normal" because he had not developed sexual feelings became a self-worth and identity issue, driven by his negative social experiences and his strong beliefs that there was something "wrong" with him. This also stirred up great feelings of anger and frustration towards others which caused him to shut down even more when he was in social situations. He had a false sense of confidence; he labeled others as "idiots," and told me he felt as though most people were far beneath him intellectually. The truth was he saw himself as "weird" and "unworthy" of other's regard because he was different and this created an avalanche of emotions, leading to his negative feelings and behaviors. His parents took him for a full battery of physical tests which revealed that his development was simply delayed, and there were no abnormalities in his endocrine system. These test results appeased him because he was very science minded and liked to have "the facts." Then I worked with him on raising his sense of self-worth through changing his self-concept through challenging negative thoughts and teaching him to deal with negative emotions. We were also able to identify people in his life who treated him well and peers who had reached out to him. Slowly, his perception of himself and the world around him began to shift and change; he began to grow emotionally and realized the feelings he thought he did not have were actually there, but he had learned to "stuff" them through denial and negative thinking.

Emotional Development during Adolescence

Anyone who has been around adolescents has probably witnessed the effects of the emotional upheaval that can be part of this journey towards adulthood. The same chemical processes that cause physical changes in the body are also responsible for causing emotional changes as well. One minute the adolescent may appear "up" and "happy" and the next minute the same adolescent may be angry, hostile, and withdrawn. If someone charted the various moods of the adolescent during a single day, one would probably see many variations. Parents often report feeling frustrated because of these variations and I meet many who become reactive towards their adolescent's mood swings. The parents I meet say things like, "I think my child is bipolar;" and "One minute everything is fine and the next minute she is crying all over the place." While chemicals are responsible for some of the emotional volatility, other factors such as brain development, emotional immaturity, and a lack of perspective also impacts the young person's emotional outbursts. I remind parents often it is not the emotions that are the problem; it is the inability of adolescents to control or modulate their reactivity when they feel the emotions hit them. This is the main part of the counseling that I do with young people, but it is difficult at times because the frontal lobes of the adolescent are still developing, and this region of the brain is helpful in controlling emotional reactivity.

I remind parents that we adults experience the same emotional "swings" but usually not to the degree or as varied as the adolescent. Part of being human is to experience emotions, but adolescence brings intensity to the experience of the emotions that at times is as confusing to the adolescent as it is to the parents and other adults who come in contact with the young person. As I wrote in the section on physical changes, I ask parents what they remember during their experience of adolescence in regards to emotional changes. I get them to think about how confusing it felt at times to have all sorts of emotions surging, and how those emotions could change without warning. Much like I wrote in that section, I think it is important for us to connect with our past in order to help us find empathy for our own adolescents as they move through this turbulent time. I find it also helps parents be non-reactive when they can remember they too experienced shifting emotional states, and I ask them to wonder what would have made it easier for them; "What could your parents have done better?" I ask. "Now, what do you think you also can do a better job of in relating to your adolescent's emotional state?" I think these are important questions to consider, not because I think it is the parent's job to "control" the young person's reactions, but to model for him or her emotional restraint is possible and that the parent can be an anchor for the adolescent during this important life stage.

Emotional Changes and the Adolescent Diagnosed with AS/HFA

The time of adolescence can be very difficult emotionally for the young person diagnosed with AS/HFA.[17] For these young people who often feel like outsiders, the onset of hormonal processes can bring about emotional upheaval that can leave them feeling even more confused and unsure of themselves. Earlier in the book I wrote about alexithymia – which is the inability to understand, identify, and give meaning to emotions in oneself and others – and how this can cause problems for the person diagnosed with AS/HFA. If you can imagine already being confused by emotions both in yourself and having difficulty interpreting the emotional state in other people, then place on top of that the emotional upheaval that occurs in adolescence and you can see what kind of problems might occur for these adolescents. There are a few other factors that make the journey of adolescence difficult for the young person diagnosed with AS/HFA when it comes to emotional development.

Emotional Immaturity

One of these factors is emotional immaturity. All adolescents regardless of being diagnosed with AS/HFA or not tend to have struggles with emotional control due to the lack of brain development in the frontal lobes that is important in being able to control emotional reactivity.[18] However, because of the challenges that come with AS/HFA, the ability of the young person to modulate or control emotional reactivity is not yet developed *and* there are the complications from years of not understanding emotions because of alexithymia. I tell parents this is the time for

---

[17] Jackson, Luke. 2002. *Freaks, geeks and asperger syndrome: A user guide to adolescence.* London England: Jessica Kingsley Publishers, 2002.

[18] Hull, K. 2011. *Play Therapy and Asperger's Syndrome: Helping Children and Adolescents Grow, Connect, and Heal through the Art of Play.* Lanham, MD: Jason Aronson.

patience because no amount of punishment, yelling, or manipulation can speed the maturation process. However, firm boundaries, structure and routine, and lots of love and connection are what the adolescent needs to get through these challenging emotional issues. I am passionate about sending this message to parents who have adolescents diagnosed with AS/HFA, and I strive to give them encouragement and remind them that being patient and focusing on connection is the best thing they can do for their children as they move through the transitions of life.

I worked with a young man about fourteen years of age diagnosed with AS/HFA who was struggling with emotional issues. His parents reported to me that he had been the target of intense bullying for some time and that he had begun to withdraw from family and activities he used to enjoy. Like many young people diagnosed with AS/HFA it took some time to build a relationship with him, but soon he was comfortable with talking with me. I remembered he liked stand-up comedians and we shared our favorite comics' moments on the stage and also talked about comedy movies and T.V. shows. Like many young people diagnosed with AS/HFA he had been a target of bullying since he began school, but he was also able to talk about some close friends that he had made along the way. He had developed some good strategies to deal with the bullying and I began to investigate his depressed mood symptoms. One of the things that came out in our talks together was this young man was feeling uncomfortable with the physical changes that had begun to happen in his body, and he was able to articulate that he felt "pressure" about becoming an adult. We must remember that many young people diagnosed with AS/HFA grow up observing life and not really partaking in it. They are present in physical form, but they often do not join in activities at a deeper level; while they are "there" they are almost like journalists on assignment who record an event but are not really partaking in the action. This young man described this phenomenon exactly as he told me about his younger years. I asked him about how he felt about sexual development and he immediately became crestfallen and stared at the floor without talking for many minutes. When he finally did speak, he paused several times, and it took him a few more minutes to put his thoughts into words which are not uncommon characteristics for many individuals diagnosed with AS/HFA, especially when talking about an uncomfortable topic.

He shared with me how thoughts about girls and sexual activity "terrified" him, and he felt "pressure" from his perceived expectations of others. He told me that to him, it seemed like people expected him to like girls, date, and assume a role that he wanted nothing to do with at this stage of his life. This was the "pressure" that he told me about, and it created a shutdown response in his behavior and mannerisms and manifested as depression. He said that his mother and her friends, as well as other family friends had made "jokes" about how he was getting to age where he would be dating and would be a "ladies man." "Got any girlfriends yet? What's wrong with you?" one family member had teased. These people had no idea how much this terrified this young man. He told me he had not experienced sexual attraction for either males or females, and this bothered him greatly; he said he was worried he was "mal-functional." Like many adolescents, he did want to talk with his parents about his feelings (he was afraid they would confront the family members and friends) and had simply allowed the depression to overtake him and the thoughts and feelings had consumed him for months. He shared with me that he had considered suicide "a few times" but wondered if the same worries and thoughts would still be with him even if he killed himself. I cannot express to you how his revelations struck my heart as I tried to grasp the pain and fear that gripped this young man, and I found myself thinking about him often between sessions as I searched for ways to encourage and comfort him.

I wanted to share this case because it is a good example of how adolescence can be a very turbulent time for young people diagnosed with AS/HFA. Like many young people like himself, this young man struggled with emotions from the time he was a small boy. When the myriad of emotions and physical changes of adolescence hit him, he became overwhelmed and did not know what to do. Thankfully, his parents were sensitive and wise enough to get him into counseling, but many parents do not. Sadly, many parents adopt a "wait and see" attitude and believe that the adolescent will grow out of his or her problems. Yet, because individuals diagnosed with AS/HFA struggle with communicating thoughts and feelings and even understanding their emotions to begin putting them into words, parents and family members assume everything is fine. I was stunned as I heard all of this pouring out of this young man, and we began working on sifting through the emotional content. I worked hard to reassure him that he was free to choose if and when he wanted to date, and also whom he wanted to date. I taught him how to change his negative thought process and by doing so showed him how he could get rid of many of the negative emotions that were plaguing him. He eventually was able to deal with the emotions he was experiencing and also learned to understand them; he also learned to put his feelings into words. As a result, his sense of self-worth increased greatly as he was able to grasp that he did not have to impress anyone or win anyone's affections; he could simply be himself and if people did not like that they could go jump in a lake.

While this young man experienced an aversion to the emotional and social expectations that adolescence can bring, another young man that I worked with who was fifteen and diagnosed with AS/HFA experienced the opposite. His parents brought him into the counseling office because he also was exhibiting symptoms of depression. However, I soon found the root of his depressed thoughts and feelings related to his desire to date, be accepted, drive a car, and literally "be cool." This young man had a strong desire to be accepted, and this was new for him. His experience of the physical and emotional upheaval of adolescence created a surge of a new desire for connection and relationship which took his parents and me by surprise, and it took him by surprise as well because he did not know what to do with all of these "new" emotions. As we began to work together, I found that he had sexual feelings, sadness, frustration, anger, as well as elation and "giddiness" all coming together into one very big vortex. His situation was complicated by the fact that since grade school he had very close friends who all happened to be girls that were always very fond of him. He suddenly found the girls very appealing and did not know what to do with the new "feelings" he was experiencing.

He had begun "acting out" in ways that were causing his peers to distance themselves from him: Saying socially inappropriate things, spreading lies, manipulating people, and lashing out angrily when people would not do what he wanted them to do. The most serious incident involved him touching a girl (who happened to be one of his friends) on the breast after she hugged him. This behavior led to school officials seeking to suspend him and the girl's parents were not happy with the young man's choices. He shared with me that it was like he no longer wanted to "hide" in the shadows. Instead, he wanted to be seen, and connect with people and be like Lady Gaga and have an entourage. To him, this seemed like something that just happened, and the idea of building relationships baffled him. I tried to help him understand the dynamics of how relationships are built and sustained, and also how someone like Lady Gaga has a great deal of money and fame that causes people to crave her company. His social and emotional difficulties stemming from AS/HFA created many barriers that made this phase of life very difficult, and counseling work with him was also very difficult! While I worked with him, I communicated with his parents to be patient and coached them to make new opportunities for him to be in social situations with family and friends as a way to fill this new need for socialization.

Both of these cases show how the emotional "overload" of adolescence can affect the young person diagnosed with AS/HFA. While both young men experienced different reactions to the onset of adolescence, both experienced the same depressed feelings as a result of the confusion of this turbulent time of life. The depressed thoughts and feelings experienced by both young men left them feeling confused and as though they had no control over their circumstances. Emotional immaturity created difficulties in these young people in that they were unable to process the emotions and understand what was going on inside them. While emotional immaturity is a common characteristic for many adolescents on the journey to adulthood, the difficulties AS/HFA can bring coupled with emotional immaturity can create long lasting difficulties and emotional wounds that could disrupt the individual's future success.

Anxiety

I have discussed earlier how anxiety is problematic for children and adolescents diagnosed with AS/HFA. Adolescents in particular struggle with anxiety and many find themselves feeling helpless against this ravaging beast. One young man shared with me that his anxiety would "knock thoughts out of my head" and he described in great detail how frustrating it was to have to "start over" and try and remember what he was thinking about just minutes before. Many researchers believe anxiety is the most difficult emotion for young people diagnosed with AS/HFA to overcome and specialized care is often needed to give young people the tools to learn to cope with this pesky emotion.[19] While anxiety does cause significant barriers in building relationship, the good news is anxiety can be overcome and I have helped many young people learn to manage anxiety and actually channel the energy it generates to positive outcomes.

I teach the young person about his or her body and how the brain works. I help the young person understand that fear is a normal part of being human and ways that he or she can manage anxiety through physical ways, such as engaging in exercise or deep breathing, as well as by learning to change thinking patterns. I also help

---

[19] Willey, Lianne Holliday. 2003. *Asperger syndrome in adolescence: Living with the ups, the downs, and things in between.* London England: Jessica Kingsley Publishers, 2003

the young person identify "triggers;" those thoughts, circumstances, or people that may invoke feelings of fear. We then dissect those triggers and examine where those triggers originated, what the triggers are connected to in the young person's environment, and the thinking patterns related to the triggers. I use many different ways to do all this; from video or computer games, art, or having the young person write a narrative of their fears and worries. All of these techniques help to make the fear become real and tangible. The anxiety takes on a form and can be looked at, created through painting or drawing, or written about. I find this is important for young people because the sooner he or she can overcome anxiety the better. Most of what people fear is not something that is actually real; it is a picture the person's mind creates of what might happen, and it is no different for young people on the autism spectrum. Once I teach the young person how fear can be overcome and ways to deal with their specific fear, he or she feels a sense of accomplishment and is better prepared to face the many life transitions that await him or her in the near future.

Increased Social Pressures and Expectations

Another factor that makes adolescence difficult for those diagnosed with AS/HFA that results in emotional difficulties is the increased social pressure and expectations that come with growing older. Most cultures naturally expect more out of young people as they grow older, and American culture is no different. By the time a young person turns eighteen in the U.S. most can drive, have had at least one part-time job, graduated high school, and have begun dating. Parents and other older adults expect the young person will find a career path or attend college to prepare for the future. These cultural expectations can create problems for those who do not fit into what society labels as "normal." However, as I remind the individuals, families, and couples that come into my counseling office, there is no "normal" and I think it is helpful to throw the term completely out the window. I have found that individuals diagnosed with AS/HFA tend to take their own path, and I rejoice with them when they do. Some may need to live at home a little longer; some may require assistance from parents and caregivers for the rest of their lives. Some may be ready to go away to college; some may need to stay closer to home.

Because many individuals diagnosed with AS/HFA tend to be bright and intuitive, I find they are often keenly aware of the expectations and demands of American society. Many that I work with share with me their feelings of despair regarding thinking they do not "fit in;" and that their future plans are not the accepted "norms" of society. I almost always find a direct correlation with this type of thinking and the feelings of sadness and despair floating around in these individuals. I work hard to help them accept the fact that their journey into adulthood and life is *their* journey, and they get to sail the waters on their own terms. But I remind them society works according to certain rules, and we must learn to navigate those rules the best that we can. I always offer the hope there is still a great deal of freedom within the operating system of social "rules" of American society.

Most people have an innate desire to "fit in" and be accepted into a group. Individuals diagnosed with AS/HFA are no different. We must remember that although many individuals diagnosed with AS/HFA have difficulties with social skills and sometimes engage in behaviors that repels others, most have a desire to connect and be loved as much as neurotypical individuals. Many adolescents and young adults diagnosed with AS/HFA with whom I work report feeling a sense of fear when they think of being independent and joining in "adult" activities. Many have difficulty seeing themselves fitting in because many have been rejected for so long by so many people; sadly, these individuals come to expect rejection in any social situation. The confusion created by a lack of understanding of emotions and social "games" often leaves adolescents terrified of marching into adulthood. I find these young people need encouragement, and they need to be able to voice their fears and worries and be reassured that they can find their way in the world and that they will be able to fit in.

I feel that I need to mention how the increased social expectations and pressure affect the parents as well as the adolescent. I encounter many parents who enter the counseling process in a frantic rush to "hurry up" and get their young person socially adjusted. When I "peel the onion," I usually find a disgruntled spouse or other family member who is putting pressure on the parent who has brought the adolescent for counseling and I remind them that society's expectations are not always the "best way" to operate, nor are society's expectations the best thing for everyone. I like to have the parent or parents look at some of the leaders and innovators throughout history in order to show them that most of the people that are revered for their accomplishments usually went "against the grain" in many ways. Some of these individuals, while being brilliant and innovative, needed other people to help them introduce their ideas to the world and they needed help in navigating the social expectations of the given society in which they live. American society is particularly annoying because there has long been a philosophy here that as long as everything looks alright on the outside, then everything must be right on the inside. American society fosters the idea there is one way to do something, one way to look, and if a person does not "fit," he or she must be "weird" and are cast out. I work hard to change parents and caregivers perspectives from a "My child needs to be changed and become normal" view to "My child is the way he is and he is special and doesn't need to be changed." I help these parents see while it helps the young person to learn how to play the social "game," it does not mean he or she needs to be changed. When young people hear that they need to be "changed," it leaves them with a feeling that they are damaged or broken, and reinforces everything that the bullies have said. I remind parents that being concerned and giving the young person the opportunity to grow and learn is one thing; sending the message that the young person is damaged and broken is quite another.

If you are a parent under pressure right now from another family member, neighbor, teacher, etc. that your adolescent diagnosed with AS/HFA needs to be changed, or if these people are filling your head with gloom and doom stories about how your child will never find his or her place in the world, please tell them you need love and encouragement and if they cannot offer that, then they are free to go on their way. I teach parents to deal with negative and judgmental family members through using the "Mary Poppins" method. In this wonderful film, Mary Poppins is confronted by an angry, frustrated Mr. Banks who criticizes her approach in teaching the children and caring for them. When he is finished blustering, Ms. Poppins kindly thanks him for his insights and tells him what a great idea it is for him to volunteer to take the children to work with him the next day. He, of course is stunned, but the next morning Mary Poppins has the children ready to go out the door, and they are very excited to get to spend the day with their still-stunned father. I call this the "Mary Poppins" method. When you as a parent, are criticized by angry/judgmental family members, listen intently and then thank them for their sincere interest, and tell them that you are glad they are willing to be part of the solution. Then, pull out your calendar and ask them which day works for them to spend time with your adolescent. Or, thank them for their generosity, and let them know how grateful you are that they would be willing to pay for counseling or an afterschool program. Try not to laugh as the person quickly disappears; or try not to fall down from surprise when they do offer help. I worked with one mother who put the "Mary Poppins" method into practice with a judgmental family member. Through this mother standing up for herself and her son, it opened up dialogue with this person and other family members. I was as surprised as this mother was by the positive outcome, and we were both grateful that family members could be educated and that they could become more active in helping this mother care for her son.

What Can Parents Do For Their Young Person Diagnosed With AS/HFA to Help Them through the Adolescent Years?

Be a "Stabilizer" and Seek to Understand

One of the concepts I stress to parents who are parenting adolescents is the idea of being a "stabilizer." Much like a large ship has stabilizers which constantly balance the vessel in times of rough water; parents must be able to be consistent, calm, non-reactive, and wise during the turbulent waters of adolescence. One way to be a stabilizer for your child is to "Seek to Understand." This means you listen without judging, without speaking, and waiting until your young person has finished his or her thought. Most young people I work with, both neurotypical and those diagnosed with AS/HFA, tell me that their parents do not really listen. I share with parents to think about how frustrating it is when a friend, neighbor, or boss sends the message that they really do not care what you are saying, but are simply waiting until you are done to slam you with their opinion. This is very frustrating! So why do we do it to our children? I find a common epidemic in our culture is the lack of listening that occurs in relationships. When parents model good listening skills with young people it helps sends the message that the parents care and, in turn, the young person feels respected. When parents of young people diagnosed with AS/HFA model listening, it is not only sending these messages but is also helping to teach the young person valuable relational skills.

Another part of "seeking to understand" is to learn as much as you can about your young person. Pretend you are Jacques Cousteau, the great explorer, on assignment in a rare, remote location and you are on assignment studying a new creature that science knows nothing about. Watch your child (the new creature) when he or she does not know you are watching. How does he behave when he is calm? When she is upset? What triggers his emotional reactions? How does she learn? How does he communicate? How does she like to spend her time? What inspires him? What career would she like to have? What kind of friends does he like? And so on and so on. All of these things that I have listed are windows into your young person's soul and represent a path to connection. And in order to learn these things, you have to listen and watch. When parents take on the role of "researcher," it helps to remove the fear and worry that often accompanies raising a young person with special needs. I encourage parents to read as much as they can about AS/HFA and to connect with other parents who have been through the same peaks and valleys. I tell parents all the time, "You are not alone!" but it is easy to feel that way. Many parents I talk to who are raising young people diagnosed with AS/HFA feel isolated and alone, misunderstood, and shunned by society. Some parents tell me they feel "left behind" as the parents of neurotypical children whiz by seemingly without a problem as the "normal" families with adolescents enter the world of dating, driving, and preparing for college or a career; while the parent of the adolescent diagnosed with AS/HFA feels "stuck" in the elementary school years.

BE A "STABILIZER" AND BATTLE DISCOURAGEMENT

Discouragement is the single greatest killer of a person's self-worth, confidence, and ability to connect in relationship. I champion the fight against discouragement everyday with individual adults, children, adolescents, couples, and families in my office. For parents especially, discouragement makes parenting that much harder because the tendency to become reactive is greater, which can cause damage to the relationship between the parent and child. This is why connection with other parents is so important, because when you realize you are not alone, you get some hope, fighting power, and patience and reassurance that your struggle is not in vain. Other parents in the struggle help you see that while things are not easy, raising a child diagnosed with AS/HFA is not just something that can be done – it can be done well. Parents must fight discouragement and fight through the despair that so often accompanies raising a child with special needs, especially in the adolescent years.

Here are some ways to fight discouragement. First, be grateful for what is going well. There may be a great deal going on that can be viewed as negative, but make a conscious choice to focus on the positive. I coach parents to find even the smallest positive, even if it is as small as a child tying his shoes by himself; celebrate that positive and look for more. A second way to battle discouragement is to ground yourself to the moment. Like I wrote earlier in the book, by staying present in the moment we are able to combat fear and worry as well as shame and guilt. A third way to battle discouragement is to be knowledgeable about your child's struggles and learn about strategies and ways to deal with the struggles. Learn parenting skills and learn about the various difficulties that young people diagnosed with AS/HFA live with on a regular basis. A fourth way to battle discouragement is to connect with other parents who are raising children and adolescents diagnosed with AS/HFA. This creates a sense of unity and togetherness and each parental unit gains a sense of power knowing that others are in the struggle and face many (if not more) of the same struggles.

Be a "Stabilizer" and Find Ways to Connect

The greatest way for a parent of a young person diagnosed with AS/HFA to provide stabilization is to find ways to connect. Despite the fact many young people diagnosed with AS/HFA tend to isolate themselves from contact with others (especially parents) as they go through turbulent waters of adolescence, I am a firm believer each young person and each parent can build connection. Keep in mind that the parent may have to accept certain limitations and lower their expectations; also keep in mind each interaction is a chance for parents to model valuable social and life skills for their young person in addition to sending the message that the adolescent is loved, cared for, and is not alone. Let us now turn our attention to the next chapter where I will discuss ways for you, the parent, to build bridges of connection with your adolescent diagnosed with AS/HFA.

Chapter 6
Techniques to Build Connection with Adolescents Diagnosed with AS/HFA

The Miracle of Playing/Connecting with Adolescents

A popular misconception about adolescents of today is that all they do is walk around with headphones jammed in their ears, watch YouTube videos, play video games, and post pictures and respond to posts on Facebook. I am here to tell you, however, that adolescents of today love to play. Granted, the forms of play at times are different than what older generations might classify as "play;" however, the context of play may have changed but the spirit is the same. I believe we all have a desire to play. We are born with it, and if left free to explore and create, we will play all day when we are young. Society tells us to stop. As we get older, guilt arises when we think of things "we ought to be doing" instead of playing; we hear the message growing up that the American version of "success" will not come if we play too much. I think this is sad. Play has the potential to help us grow, heal, and connect with others in unique ways. Play helps our brains release endorphins that help to ward off stress and depression.

For adolescents diagnosed with AS/HFA, play can take on many forms. Because of emotional immaturity, some adolescents enjoy playing with toys and games that are designed for children much younger. However, some adolescents diagnosed with AS/HFA "play" with mechanical devices, electronics, or engines that have a practical purpose. Some appear to not have the desire to "play" at all. It is quite a mixture when it comes to the topic of play and adolescents diagnosed with AS/HFA; I remind parents of Forrest Gump's famous quote, "You never know what you are going to get." However, I have yet to find a young person who did not have an interest in *something*! And it is in this "something" that parents and caregivers have an opportunity to build connection with the young person and get into his or her world. This chapter will help you as a parent find ways to connect and to also learn to deal with the feelings of rejection that all parents of adolescents feel from time to time, but especially parents of adolescents diagnosed with AS/HFA.

How Do I Play/Connect with my Teenager?

This is a common question I am often asked by parents and caregivers. I wrote earlier in the book how many adults have long forgotten how to play and sadly, some were not given many opportunities to do so as a child or were told by parents, teacher, and other authority figures that play was "bad." For parents of adolescents, they often feel an invisible wall of rejection from their adolescent; it is as if there is a "force-field" around the young person that says "Get away from me; I don't want you close to me". I encourage parents to push through this imaginary wall, and it is imaginary. Usually the wall is made up of the parent's sense of insecurity, self-doubt, and fear of rejection. For adolescents diagnosed with AS/HFA, it is often difficult for them to put their feelings into words and while they desire closeness with parents and other family members, it is very hard if not impossible for them to communicate their feelings effectively. Remember "play" with adolescents begins by making yourself available and showing an interest in what they find interesting. It means shifting into the role of observer and researching and learning to "just be." It also means pushing aside insecurity, the fear of rejection, and the fear of looking foolish.

Make Yourself Available

The first step in connecting with your adolescent diagnosed with AS/HFA is making yourself available. While this seems very simplistic, let me ask you a question to bring this into focus. How much time do you spend per day with your adolescent in one-on-one quality time? Quality time means that you are completely focused on your child, with no computer, TV, phone, or other distraction getting in the way. How much time do you spend per week watching the shows he likes, sitting with him and asking him about his day and sharing about your day? Here are some more questions. What is her favorite movie, book, or TV show? Who are her friends? What music does she like, and more specifically, what is her favorite song *right now*? What career would he like to have some day? Who inspires him, who are his heroes? What would be the perfect day to him? What is her most prized possession? What does she like to spend money on? I could go on with many more. How did you do? Were you able to answer these questions? If not, you have some work to do! By the way, I challenge myself with these questions from time to time when I think about how well I connect with my children, and sometimes I realize that I too have work to do in this area.

My point is we often expect our children to adapt to our world. This is because we are lazy and selfish if the truth be told. It takes work to adapt to their world and it takes consistent commitment, sacrifice, and focus. Many parents of adolescents I work with make comments like "I don't play video games;" "I would feel silly playing LEGO® with my son;" "I can't stand the music she listens to;" I don't get the TV shows he likes;" I don't like to read the types of books my daughter likes;" "He likes to be outside and it's just too hot for me;" "He watches wrestling on Monday nights and I think that is ridiculous;" "She is just not like me and we don't have anything in common." Do you see a common theme running through these comments? If you said "selfishness" you are exactly right. This is not because parents purposely want to ignore their adolescents and ruin the relationship with their young person, it is mainly because our lives as adults are so busy that by the time our children can feed themselves and dress themselves we gradually "check out" because of how tired many of us have become. We are grateful when our adolescents can "entertain themselves." Please know that I am not saying we need to be in our adolescents' lives every minute of every day. I believe in balance and giving our young people free time to themselves is also positive and healthy. However, when it comes to building connection, especially with parents of adolescents diagnosed with AS/HFA, I find most parents have some work to do.

Making ourselves available means we are presenting ourselves to our adolescent in a complete way. This is the idea that nothing is in the way when you sit down to spend time with your child. Your presence is saying to him, "I am here to be with you and I am all yours." I tell parents (and myself) that this means we put down the phone, close the laptop, and eliminate all distractions. I challenge you to make this happen every day and watch the differences your behavior begins to make. By the way, a mere fifteen minutes will do just fine. Many parents believe to spend quality time with their young person means carving out hours; I like to remind them to make just fifteen minutes per day their goal. Usually they breathe a sigh of relief as they realize making themselves available is not as gargantuan a task as previously thought.

For parents of adolescents diagnosed with AS/HFA, the concept of "making yourself available" is very important for several reasons. First, it is hard for young people diagnosed with AS/HFA to put thoughts/feelings into words. Their behavior might be saying, "I'm fine. I don't need you to spend time with me," but inside they may be feeling very empty and alone. I have witnessed firsthand in my office the shock on parent's faces when they hear how much the young person wants her parent(s) to be more involved in her life. A second reason why making yourself available is important with adolescents diagnosed with AS/HFA is that it sends the message through your behavior that your adolescent is important and valuable. Remember that many of these remarkable young people go through childhood and adolescence believing that others do not like them and that they are not valuable enough to be noticed, yet they long for connection with others. Parents provide a sense of stability against these negative beliefs when they consistently make an effort to be present in their young person's life. A third reason why making yourself available is so powerful is that you, as the parent, are able to model valuable relationship skills through your behavior. Children and adolescents diagnosed with AS/HFA need to see socially appropriate behavior modeled, and when you as a parent continue to send the message that "You are valuable" by making time for them, the young person is able to see an important ingredient in both building and sustaining a relationship.

Get Rid of Insecurity!

Let's face it: adolescents can be intimidating creatures. Their reactions and behavior can make you think you are dumb, insignificant, and worthless. When I first began working with young people at a local Children's home, my first duty was to sit with adolescent boys after school for homework time. I introduced myself, and not one of the adolescent boys spoke. I then tried to get conversation going by asking questions but no one spoke to me. I remember a feeling of helplessness creep over me; my mind raced to think of something to "hook" them with and get them talking, anything; something that would make me look cool and likeable. The harder I tried the more nothing happened. The air was thick with a feeling of awkwardness; they were probably as uncomfortable as I was. I remember leaving the room feeling absolutely foolish and completely humbled. While none of the boys had said a word, I felt as though I had been hit with a giant club. This experience was valuable because I learned to not try so hard and just be myself. My training also taught me most adolescents are very insecure because of all the physiological, cognitive, and emotional changes that are going on. I learned to be non-reactive and to present a stable and consistent manner of talking and interacting with them. I that learned no matter what you do, adolescents are going to see you as "weird" and "annoying," it comes with the landscape so we might as well get used to it.

Parents of adolescents diagnosed with AS/HFA struggle with insecurity because many of them have felt rejected and disowned by their child for a long time. Adolescents diagnosed with AS/HFA have trouble putting feelings into words, handling emotions, and seeing things from another person's perspective; as a result, these young people often erupt at the slightest irritation. These eruptions usually occur in the home and around parents and caregivers, which triggers the "fight-or-flight" response in the parent and results in yelling, hurtful words, and withdrawing behavior. This creates a cycle of discouragement and insecurity in the parent and further reinforces to the young person that they are a "misfit." So how can a parent get rid of insecurity? It all begins with changing your thoughts and perspective. First, parents must resist the urge to save or fix their child. This is done through seeing the gifts that come with AS/HFA, celebrating those gifts, seeing the adolescent as a miracle and being in complete wonder at who this young person is. This means parents must stop comparing the young person to other young people and throw out the cultural/social expectations, and accept their child's limitations but also the young person's gifts and talents. Trust me; those gifts and talents are there if we dare look. I cannot tell you how many times in my office the immense weights are lifted off parents and caregivers' backs when they grasp the concept of daring to shed societal and cultural expectations and simply focusing on building connection.

A second way of battling insecurity through changing thinking and perspective is to see the task of parenting a young person with AS/HFA as a long journey. Remember how the pioneers travelled to the west? It was long, slow, and sometimes very difficult. This is the landscape of parenting a young person diagnosed with AS/HFA: long, slow, and sometimes difficult. However, there are many miracles along the way and patience is a key element. When parents shift their mindset to see a young person's development as a long journey, it helps relieve the pressure that there is a "finish line" or think that it is a race to get the young person to some imaginary destination. This is a myth; the journey of parenting really never ends, and while the context and details of the parenting changes and new challenge arise, the relationship and connection aspects never change. This is why I am so passionate about connection and relationship because this is the solid foundation on which everything else rests! See your parenting of your adolescent diagnosed with AS/HFA as a long journey and be in the moment, the miracle of now!

This brings up a third way to get rid of insecurity and changing your thinking and perspective: *Be in the moment!* I know you have heard this already from me, but this helps ward off insecure thoughts of doubting yourself and thinking you are not "good enough" for this task of parenting. Do this right now. Relax your stomach and simply take in everything around you in this moment. See that you have clothing, shelter, and probably have eaten something in the last few hours. Live in abundance of this moment and notice right now you have the skills to connect with your child/children in this moment; see that in this moment you are perfect. Our brains want us to be safe and feel connected so we imagine the worst thing happening in the future (FEAR) and then we think about all our failures of the past (SHAME, REGRET) and that sucks the life out of now. Do not let this happen! Embrace the miracle of this moment; be grateful for what is good in this moment; and see yourself as capable and competent. You are reading this book in this moment and as I am writing this in this moment I am envisioning a discouraged parent who is grasping for help. See that even now, in this moment, you are doing something to make yourself smarter and better equipped for this journey. I am so glad you just did this little exercise: practice staying in the moment and you will find you are better able to control negative thoughts and emotions.

Model Play and Connection in Your Life

There is an interesting phenomenon that happens as we raise our children. When they are young, they tend to like what we like and like to do what they see us doing. Many young children want to "be" what mom or dad does for a career, because they see it and come to know all about it. If dad is into golf, his children will more than likely be interested in golf. If a mom sews, or plays tennis, her children will probably like the same things. While the specific interest does not always "stick" as the children get older, what does stick is that children who see their parents be passionate about something will understand that healthy adults have diverse interests in which they involve themselves. This phenomenon also applies to academics; children who see their parents reading and learning and see books in the house get the idea that reading and learning is something that everyone does. This phenomenon also applies to social settings; children who see their parents connecting with others get the idea of a social world outside of the immediate family and home.

What do your children see you doing for fun? What activities do you engage in which shows your passion and interest? Is there something that inspires you that your children see you pursuing? Do you share your favorite type of music with them? Do they know your favorite movie? Do they see you sacrificing your time and effort towards something worthwhile like a college degree or training that will better yourself in some way? How can we expect our children to want to strive, learn, grow, and connect with others if they get the idea that all we do is work, sit on the couch, watch TV, and go to bed day after day? Please know that I am not advocating being so busy and involved in so many things that we appear to our young people like hamsters on a wheel. What I am saying is that parents should be modeling something in their lives that shows that you play and have specified interests too. This helps us appear human, touchable, and real. This helps us fight off stress and renews our energy to keep striving and connecting with our children. We appear diversified, competent, and professional. Adolescents diagnosed with AS/HFA needs to see the modeling of such behavior from parents and caregivers, as this creates a picture for them of what a healthy individual looks like. I challenge you to find a passion and let yourself play. Give yourself permission to do something for yourself; allow your adolescent to be a part of it and share your interests with him or her and then model being involved and connected to that interest or passion. This modeling is very important for your adolescent diagnosed with AS/HFA.

Building Bridges with Adolescents through Play and Connecting

Many of these concepts and ideas will be the same as in the section on connecting with children but the techniques will be different because I have adapted them for adolescents. Much of what you are going to read are the same techniques that I use with families in my office and I know them to be very effective in creating closer connections between parents/caregivers and the adolescent diagnosed with AS/HFA.

Using the Adolescent's Specified Interest as a Pathway to Connection

I believe in this so strongly that I have included it in both the section related to children and this section. Young people diagnosed with AS/HFA usually have a specified interest that consumes their time and energy. Does your adolescent have a specified interest? If they do, it is a wonderful way to connect with them and find out more about how they think, what they feel, and to build a stronger connection with them. One young man I worked with who was about thirteen was really into a computer game and played it constantly. His father and mother felt frustrated because they told me they did not know how to get the young man interested in anything else. I shared with them the intense focus of an individual diagnosed with AS/HFA on something they find interesting is difficult if not impossible to change, and I asked if they thought about using the game to connect with the young man. They both appeared shocked and told me they did not think that would work. When I inquired as to why they believed that, they told me that "We don't play computer games." I asked if they had read about the game ("No") and if they had ever researched the details of the game ("No") and if they ever pulled up a chair and sat with him while he played. "Well, he doesn't seem to mind but he just sits there and does not talk to us, so we assumed he didn't want us there." I knew from speaking with the young man that he did not mind them sitting there at all; in fact, he enjoyed the attempt that they made to inquire about the game but he did not communicate this fact to his parents.

Thankfully, these parents took my suggestions to heart and began to spend more and more time with their son sitting with him when he played the game, and the father even made an account and started to play online himself. The boy was ecstatic as he was able to show his father all about his imaginary world he loved so much and it created a wonderful bond. These parents found things out about their son they did not know before and the young man found things out about his parents. The parents found that the game contained themes of social connection including forming social groups, working together, and making future plans. I want to point out in this situation the parents had to step outside their comfort zones and push through feeling uncomfortable in order to do this. We humans are creatures of habit, and many of the roles we play in personal relationships and our families are simply habits that form almost unconsciously. For these parents, a pattern of behavior formed when they saw their son playing his computer game: *Leave him alone and do not speak to him.* For the son: *I am playing my game and mom and dad will not speak to me or associate with me.* The parents however, pushed through this and formed a new pattern that created an opening for relationship around playing the game. I celebrated their success and praised the young man for being open to this new pattern of interacting with his parents.

A fourteen year old girl diagnosed with AS/HFA was referred to me for depression and suicidal thinking. She was a lover of art and was very good at drawing and graphic design. While her parents knew this and encouraged her in her pursuit of art, there was something missing. From my perspective, her parents did not connect with her in her art, and I encouraged them to begin to join her in her drawing and to let her teach them about what she could do on the computer. Both of the parent's initial reaction was the same: "We don't draw." I told them that I understood, but I believed that it would help their daughter if they made an effort to connect with her through the art and show an interest. This young lady's depression and suicidal thinking soon diminished as her parents made an effort to connect deeper with her through her love of art. I share these examples because both sets of these parents were not naturally drawn to what their children loved. However, by branching out, changing their perspective, and making a conscious effort, both of these families reaped the reward of closer connection and the chance to model for their adolescent the power of building relationship.

Computer/Video Games

I wrote earlier about how useful computer and video games can be in the therapy process as well as in building connection between parents/caregivers and children diagnosed with AS/HFA, but I also wanted to include it in the section with adolescents because I feel it is very important. Adolescents diagnosed with AS/HFA seem naturally drawn to the computer and computer games. Computers represent neat ordered systems and operate on a foundation of rules that individuals diagnosed with AS/HFA tend to be drawn to, and the games that are played on the computer and video game consoles also are built on a foundation of rules and order. Today's technology enables a player of a computer or video game to be in the online environment and play the game with people all over the world, another draw for the young person diagnosed with AS/HFA. I have met many who tell me that connecting with others through online gaming has helped them branch out socially in the "real" world. I help parents see that this medium can be a wonderful way to learn how your adolescent thinks, strategizes, connects, and sees the world.

Many parents of adolescents I work with feel lost when it comes to connecting with their young person through computer/video games for several reasons. Many of the games that adolescents play are very complex with detailed patterns of play. Many are designed for only one player who connects through the online world to other players. Some of the games have content that parents do not find appealing; in fact, some find the content very offensive and wish to not sit and be exposed to the violence, blood, etc. Yet another reason is that some young people view the game play as "their world" and feel uncomfortable when a parent or family member wants to sit and watch them play. However, I encourage parents that while it may seem daunting to try to connect, there are several ways that this can be done.

Communication and Asking "Open-Ended" Questions about Video/Computer Games

Parents of adolescents diagnosed with AS/HFA often remark to me that they do not know "where to start" when it comes to connecting with their young person through a computer/video game. I tell them to begin with information. Ask questions, but not just any question I tell them. I advise using "open-ended" questions; that is, questions that elicit more information than just "yes" or "no" answers. A closed question is designed to only get a one word answer. ("Did you have a good day at school?" "Yes".) Here is how it works: Pretend I am the parent and I want to talk to my son about the computer game that he loves.

Parent: "Hey Jon, I notice you really like _____ and you play it a lot. Could you tell me about the game?"

This question began with a statement which contained an observation and then the question was an opening for more information. A "yes" or "no" (closed response) is not appropriate here because it does not match the question. My question is phrased in a way that communicates to Jon that I want detailed information and in bulk form. Here is how Jon's response is likely to go:

Jon: "Ok, well, it is a game about the future in a far off galaxy that takes place between three different planets."

Notice that Jon's response is detailed and full of information that tells me quite a lot. His response also sets up more questions that I can ask that can get more information as well. This is another value of the open-ended question format. Let us seen how this might evolve from here:

Parent: "Wow. Sounds like a pretty cool story, I want to know more. Can you tell me about the objectives of the game?"

Jon: "Sure. Well, you have to establish a colony on one of the planets and then try to defeat the enemy forces that inhabit the other two. You only have a limited number of people and supplies, so you have to be smart in not running out of resources and be able to create weapons at the same time."

Once again, there is more information given that is both explanatory and detailed and as a parent this is what I am looking for. I do not want to "close" this dialogue. As we are talking there are several things happening. One is Jon is learning to trust me because I am sending the message that I care about what interests him. Another is I am showing genuine interest and am sincerely interested in getting in his world. A third occurrence is through open-ended questioning I am making an *invitation* for him to tell me; there is no interrogation or demand for information. Fourth, I am modeling how good conversation is both initiated and maintained. Let us continue to play out this conversation and imagine where it might go.

Parent: "Sounds like a lot of work, but it also seems fun. I can see where this takes a long time to play. No wonder you don't like it when Mom and I spring something on you and make you have to stop playing! Can you tell me what you like about the game?"

Notice that I have now shifted the question from information about the game to something personal for Jon to share. If I asked him this right off the bat, it may have caught him off guard and he may not have shared anything, or tried to give the classic adolescent response "I don't know" (shoulder shrug).

Jon: "Well, it's like my own world, you know? Like, I can create a world and I'm in charge of planning strategies, and creating weapons, and fighting battles. I really like how it's my own thing…my own world."

Jon has now given me personal information connected to the game. I can begin to understand he likes being in charge of something and this game provides a sense of joy that comes from competence as well as having something he views as completely his. From finding out about what he likes about the game, I am able to generalize this to how Jon sees the world. This is the power of this approach and what I wrote about in my dissertation regarding the use of computer/video games to better understand how a young person thinks and sees the world through the games they play and how he or she plays them.

At this point in the conversation, I have a number of choices in talking with Jon about the game. I could continue to ask him more detailed questions about the game or I could also continue to use the information to get Jon to open up about his personal life based on what he has told me about the game. I will show you how this can be done.

Parent: "So it gives you a sense of being in control and being in charge. Do you like feeling this way in everyday life?"

Jon: "Yeah, I guess I do."

Parent: "Can you tell me if you feel like this very often, you know, like when you are at school?"

Jon: "Well…I have a hard time. I mean, it seems like life doesn't really work that way. I mean, like at school, I don't feel like I'm in charge of anything…it seems like I am always being told where to go and what to do".

Parent: "So that's why you like the game so much."

Jon: "Yeah…it makes me feel good."

Jon's feelings about everyday life about how he feels in "everyday life" are significant and help the parent understand a little bit about what daily life brings for Jon. I hope you can now appreciate in a new way not only how to use communication and more importantly open-ended questions in getting your adolescent to open up about the computer/video game that he or she loves, but also how important games are in the lives of these remarkable young people.

PULL UP A CHAIR AND WATCH

Have you ever pulled up a chair and watched your adolescent play the computer/video game he loves? If you have, I applaud you and encourage you to keep doing it. Most parents I encounter, however, rarely sit and watch their adolescent engage in computer/video game play. I encourage this because it sends the message to the young person that you are willing to enter his world. Your action of sitting with him, tells him that you care, you are interested, and you are willing to learn about what he is passionate about. I get all kinds of responses from parents on this, from "I don't have time" to "He would think I'm crazy." My response is always the same; "Young people diagnosed with AS/HFA need to know that parents are willing to go the extra mile for them, even if they don't always say it or show it." Parents often want to know, "What do I say?" or "What do I do?" and my response is always the same. "Just be, and let what happens happen." Usually I get a look of baffled confusion at this point. When people think of sitting in silence and not saying anything, panic usually sets in. However, I have found people diagnosed with AS/HFA are quite comfortable with silence, and I think it is a wonderful attribute to have.

I have become accustomed to the world of silence because many of the young people I work with who are diagnosed with AS/HFA are not very verbal. When I ask them a question, it may take them a few minutes to respond. I have learned over the years that if I just "chill," I will get an answer and silence is just fine. No one dies; in fact, it is quite liberating. Two people sitting together in each other's presence can communicate a great deal, and verbal interaction is just a fraction of that interaction. However, we live in a culture that values unnecessary noise and constant talking. I would love to someday be able to just watch a football game or basketball game on TV without a commentator telling me what the quarterback was thinking when he threw the interception or what was running through a point guard's mind when he did not find the open player to shoot the last second shot. What if it was just the sound of the players on the field and the crowd cheering? Can you imagine? No, that day will never come because here in America we must be lectured on every tiny thing from sports, to finances, to how to grow herbs. How in the world did our founding fathers make it without the Today Show telling them what to do? How could Abraham Lincoln have made his decisions without CNBC informing him of what tie the Egyptian diplomat was going to wear that day?

My point is what we miss in our culture is that yes, relationships do require verbal communication, but relationships also need silence. Much like the gaps in music makes the mind interpret the music as beautiful, silence during conversation makes that conversation meaningful. My other point is too much talking can confuse young people diagnosed with AS/HFA. Many times, their brains take in so much information at one time that if there is not a pause to collect it all, sift through it, organize a response, and a pause while they deliver that response, relationships can be very scary for these amazing individuals. Sitting and watching your adolescent play her favorite game is an opportunity for you to be silent and "just be." Simply sit and absorb the action and watch and see what happens. Get rid of an "agenda" of what you think should happen and resist the urge to speak or make something happen. Trust me, "just be" and good things will happen!

GIVE PLAYING THE GAME A TRY!

Many parents that I encounter simply have rarely played computer or video games and this is the cause of their fear in engaging in game play. "I might fail;" "I will feel foolish;" and "There are too many buttons" are many of the excuses that I hear. I encourage them to give the game a try and tell them this is wonderful way to connect with their adolescent and also demonstrate a different side of their personality to their adolescent. I firmly believe when we set aside our "stuff" (fears, insecurities, etc.) for the sake of connecting with our young person, good things happen on many levels. The first positive is the parent is modeling the behavior of trying something new and different. Individuals diagnosed with AS/HFA often have specified interests that keep them from trying something new or different; many have a hard time considering trying something that they see as "outside their box." This characteristic often limits individuals diagnosed with AS/HFA as they transition from adolescence into adulthood because they have a hard time finding a career that includes characteristics of things they do not like or enjoy. I work very hard with the young people I meet with in trying to get them to see that nobody likes every part of their job; no matter how much people love their work there is at least some minute detail that most people find oppressive or unpleasant. While I love counseling individuals and helping people and families solve problems, I do not like the administrative paperwork and report writing that often accompanies what I do. However, it is only a small part of the helping piece that I find so enjoyable. Individuals diagnosed with AS/HFA often struggle with trying new things but when they see mom or dad try something, they get the idea that they can also.

A second positive from the parent trying to play a computer/video game is by placing the young person in the role of teacher and the parent in the role of the pupil. Why is this so powerful, you may ask? We forget as adults that our children rarely get to teach us anything. While society bemoans the fact that adolescents seem more and more immature, it does not occur to many people we have limited their opportunities to "step up" and shine. Yet, there is a lot young people can teach us if we allow time for the teaching and let them step up and shine. One of the "perks" of my work is that kids and adolescents teach me all sorts of things. I know about the latest buzz words, latest fads, what is "cool" and what "isn't cool," what musician and music is on the rise and what actor, actress, or show is on the way out. I know how to make things, how things work; I know cheat codes and bypass links for games and electronic devices. Sadly, I know how overwhelmed and underappreciated our young people feel and how afraid they are of the future. My point is by making the time and encouraging your child, he or she will gladly teach you things, and this is important because it not only forges a new respect and relationship, but it helps that young person feel valued, loved, and needed. For adolescents diagnosed with AS/HFA, letting their parent into their world of computer/video games can be the beginning of a new relationship and give the parent an opportunity to connect with the young person on a deeper level.

I find that young people diagnosed with AS/HFA know a great deal, especially about something they are very interested in. However, I find they are rarely invited to teach others about what they know. Because of the tendency in those diagnosed with AS/HFA to avoid people and relationships, others around them do not realize the individual is an "expert" in whatever area their specialized interest is. Families and parents have heard about the interest for so long that they sometimes become accustomed to the stream of knowledge that flows out of the individual diagnosed with AS/HFA and sometimes, sadly, tend to see the person as a nuisance. However, I have witnessed a powerful phenomenon of connection and growth when the parents and young people I work with allow themselves to be taught about the video/computer game the adolescent loves. This once happened with a single mother who always viewed the video game playing of her son as "annoying" and something that she "just didn't understand." As he became an adolescent, the landscape of his life became littered, as it often does for young people diagnosed with AS/HFA with bullying, low self-worth, talk of suicide, and a general sense of melancholy settled over him and their home. In addition to beginning working with him on raising his self-worth and teaching him skills to deal with negative emotions and the bullying, I focused on the connection between him and his mother. She shared with me that she had "let him do his own thing" when they were together at home in the last few years because she said it seemed as though "he didn't need me" in the same way and stopped asking to do things together. She explained she cooked dinner and watched her shows, and he stayed in the computer room and played his games. As we were discussing her building a connection with him during this phase of his life, I asked her, "What has been the constant in his life through all of what he has been experiencing; what is something that he has continued to do and loves?" She replied it was his games he played on the computer. It dawned on her the games had become his "safe place;" the games were what stabilized him and he could be in his "own world," and be in charge of his world. She renewed her commitment to connect with him and used the games as a way to make this happen. She researched about the games, learned about them, watched him play, and allowed him to teach her about the games. At first he was taken aback by her desire to watch him play and to learn about "his world", but then he became delighted to teach her once he realized she was serious in her commitment to connect with him. This case inspired me to continue to encourage parents to branch out and learn about the computer/video games that their young people love so much.

FINDING METAPHORS IN COMPUTER/VIDEO GAMES

I explained earlier in the book that play is very useful in the therapy process because it can help a child heal, find meaning in a difficult experience, and finally, play can give the therapist valuable tools in teaching the child or adolescent. One way a therapist can help a child through play is finding metaphors in the play of the child or adolescent. Computer/video games provide wonderful metaphors for overcoming problems that adolescents encounter in real life; as someone who uses play therapy on a regular basis I look for these metaphors when I play computer/video games with young people or when they show me a game they love. I find adolescents diagnosed with AS/HFA are often drawn to the computer/video game world because it allows them to be in charge which serves to create a sense of safety which comes from being in control. I explain this to parents who are frustrated with the amount of time their young person spends play a game. I help them see the "obsession" is related to feeling safe and being in control; for these young people this is very important because these feelings can be built upon and generalized to the real world. This is the power of creating metaphors from the game, and the hope is that the young person will apply what is learned through the game to situations that are encountered in everyday life.

The first step in this process is looking for themes in the game such as overcoming obstacles, working with other to achieve goals, and going to new levels. There are character trait themes that are found in the games also such as perseverance, patience, sharing, goal setting, and thinking strategies. One of the joys of my work is when I help young people with little self-confidence see that what they encounter in playing a video game is really the exact same situation that they are facing in real life. "If you can do it in the game, you can do it in real life" I tell them. I have witnessed this over and over in my work and have seen this truth help many young people become stronger and adept in navigating social situations, as well as learn to effectively deal with bullies and build up their sense of value and worth. I tell parents once these themes are identified they can begin teaching their adolescent to be aware of relating these to their life outside of the game.

The second step in this process is teaching the young person how to apply the themes from the game play to real life. This step requires connection (the parent must understand and know the themes of the game and watch the adolescent play) and imagination (being aware of the real life experiences and thinking of how to make the application from game to real life. This is what a play therapist does with the themes that emerge from the play session with a child. Some parents doubt themselves when I introduce this concept to them; however, I reassure them that with a little training, they too can learn to see these themes and look for places in the child's personal life where they can be applied. Because I am passionate that parents are and should be the greatest teachers their children will ever encounter, I help this become a reality, especially with parents raising children on the autism spectrum. I will help illustrate this second step through sharing a real-life case in which a parent learned to teach valuable skills in addition to building connection.

Brian and the Bullies

Brian was an adolescent plagued by bullies. This problem caused a great deal of emotional and mental strain, and created stress for his mother as well. His mother, a single mother for much of Brian's life, was concerned that the bullying would drive Brian further into isolation. He, like many young people diagnosed with AS/ HFA was attached to electronic devices from about the time he learned to walk and his mother was convinced that his "obsession" with computer/video games was "ruining" his life. This thinking was based on Brian's intense game play and his intense withdrawal from social interactions. Prior to coming to see me, his mother had embarked on a campaign to get Brian to stop playing them and help him "branch out into other interests." I listened with an inner grin as she told me how this failed miserably, in fact, she told me, "I think I made him like computer and video games even more as a result of my efforts, and we went through a time where it seemed we hated each other." I suggested that she make an effort to join Brian in the game play, through sitting and watching, reading about the games he likes, and seeing if there was a way to use what he did in the game play that could be applied to the "real-life" situation involving the bullies. She was open-minded to this idea and was willing to learn. Like any good parent, she desperately wanted to mend the relationship with Brian and also be a force in teaching him valuable life skills.

We began by looking at the types of games that Brian liked to play. There was one particular role-playing game that he played online with many other players. His mother surmised this game took up most of his time and from what he had told her, he was very good at it. She told me when she threatened to take this game away from him and limit his playing time, he had threatened killing himself if he had to live life without being able to play the game. I reassured her that this is a common reaction, especially for individuals diagnosed with AS/HFA. For Brian, the thought of not having his game was like living without air or food. I gave her "homework" which involved researching about the game and learning to understand the dynamics of the game. I also encouraged her simply to "just be" and watch her son play the game. She was nervous about this, but agreed to pull up a chair next to him: "He'll think I'm nuts, but I'll give it a try." This mother followed all of the recommendations that I put in the previous section and gradually she gained an understanding of the game her son loved to play. I also helped her look for "themes" that were embedded in the game that were similar to Brian's struggles in everyday life. She was amazed to see themes of confidence, conquering, working with others, frustration, strategic planning, and thinking through problems. She was also amazed at his ability to communicate with others, which he did through wearing a headset. She found out that he had formed deep relationships with the people he played with regularly and he knew a great deal about them; she was also surprised to hear him offering encouragement, sympathy, and laugh with those with whom he played: "I cannot believe that I thought he was just sitting in the computer room on that game night after night just wasting his time; turns out, he is developing into an amazing young man!"

I become very excited when I hear parents say this; it rejuvenates me in my work to continue teaching, encouraging, and modeling for parents to look for and find hidden "nuggets" in their young person's character and abilities they did not see before embarking on this journey of discovery. This mother was able to see the why of the draw of the games for Brian; it finally began to make sense why he was so consumed with playing the game. She discovered themes in the game that he enjoyed: Themes of creating alliance, strategizing, sheer power and force, commitment, and sacrifice. She noticed her son would work very hard to gain something he thought was important and she found herself refraining from thinking of him as "lazy." She began to see if he did not think a task was important, like writing a history paper or cleaning his room, he did not want to put effort towards it. This helped her in finding new ways to help motivate him towards doing things he did not like; and instead of lecturing him and belittling him for not doing daily tasks which he found unpleasant and mundane, she found ways to partner with him in tasks to show that she did not like them either, but showed him that the tasks needed to be done as this is a necessary part of life.

The next step in the process was helping Brian's mother take the themes that she identified in the game and helping Brian generalize these themes to his real life situations. As I wrote earlier, this requires imagination. Two themes that Brian's mother identified was using the socializing that he did in the game and applying this to real-life social situations. The other was using the strengths in the game to help Brian stand up to the bullies. Part of Brian's difficulties with the bullies was he did not know how to stand up to them, which made him feel cowardly and weak. This cycle contributed to his perception that people were "not safe" and influenced his hermit-like behavior. I remind people that for individuals diagnosed with AS/HFA, it is not that they do not want connection with others; it is simply because they do not always know how to make it happen. I instructed her to help Brian understand that he needed to connect with the feeling of power and competence that he got out of playing the game to the real-life situation of standing up to the bullies and not letting them push him around. Brian's mother noticed that there were several parts in the game where Brian not only stood up for himself, but also attacked other "rival" groups that were infringing on his territory. An imaginary bell "dinged" in her head: She had a remarkable idea. She realized if she could get Brian to view the real-life situation with the bullies in the same way he approached the game, he would have more confidence to face the situation and perhaps not suffer so much emotional damage.

This phase of using metaphors created from computer/video games not only requires imagination but also communication. The parent must be able to communicate this to the adolescent and do it in a way that the young person grasps the idea and is able to see a connection. Sometimes this takes a few tries and the parent must be patient at this stage. This is the "meat" of the therapeutic work that I do and it can be challenging for me despite my years of training and practice. For this to work, I must be patient, non-reactive, and willing to try different ways of communicating with the young person. If the parent gets frustrated because the young person is not "getting it" and reacts negatively, the young person may shut down and become resistant to talking about the situation. This is why consistent relationship is so important; it helps the young person reframe the parent's attempts at communication from being intrusive and annoying to teaching and guiding. Brian's mother established a pattern in which she learned about his game, spent time watching him, and opened up new patterns of communication with Brian. This process evolved over a period of two to three months. She began to talk with Brian about the bullies and asked him what he would do if he encountered them in the game. "I would slay them no problem" he replied confidently. She explored his thoughts and feelings related to this, and he told her that in the game he feared no one, and fully believed that he could take on anyone in a battle. It was time for the golden question.

Mom: "What if you approached the bullies in the same way, I wonder what that would look like," she asked in a curious manner.

Brian: "MOM! I can't go cut their heads off! GEEZ!" Brian retorted, looking at her like she needed to be institutionalized.

Mom: "I know that," she responded calmly, "But imagine approaching them with no fear, feeling confident, and believing that you are not going to die and that they are not better than you."

Brian: "Yeah, I guess, but I feel like I can't stand up to them because there is more of them and I don't have any real fighting skills. I mean, in the game I have weapons and a set of battling skills that I have worked on for years. Besides, it's different in real life...I guess I'm just destined to be treated like this."

This is a key point in the dialogue as Brian is expressing his feelings of helplessness at the reality of the situation. What I coach parents to do here is to remember that it is not their job to "fix" the situation for the child or adolescent, but to give them a different perspective and open dialogue to new ways of thinking and skills that can help the young person face the problem or situation. The sad truth of our world is that we will encounter bullies for the rest of our lives and we must learn to stand up to people who want to take advantage of us, and I am a firm believer teaching our children to believe in themselves and not be afraid to stand up for their rights and go to people for help. A big problem in our world is parents solving their children's problems for them and believing that they must "pave the path" for the child. I remind parents that they must "hand the problem back" to the child or adolescent and give them tools and skills to navigate their world. Individuals diagnosed with AS/HFA tend to blame themselves when they encounter negative social experiences and they tend to view themselves as "bad" or "worthless" because of the rejection of others. They tend to do the same thing with negative emotions ("I'm feeling sad because I am worthless"). These cycles tend to keep the person in a state of isolation and despair. Because Brian's mother is wise, she takes what he has said and offers an alternative without rushing to fix the problem:

Mom: "What do you think it would take to stand up to them?"

Brian: "I would need to be able to fight in real life, and that's not going to happen unless I start Judo or something like that."

Mom: "We could enroll you in a martial arts class; there is one right up the street and I think you could go after school. You know, the confidence that you have in the game comes from realizing who you are as a person…and that you are smart and have something to offer the world. Look at how your fellow players like you! I am amazed at how you get along so well with them. I think the bullies would be shocked if you stood up to them and told them not to push you around. Would you like to get enrolled in a martial arts class?"

Brian: "Yeah I think I would. It would be nice to try…I just don't like to feel helpless. I would like to know that I could protect myself if I needed to."

Mom: "Ok, I can do that for you, and I will go with you if you want me to. But I want you to think about how confident you are in your game and that you can be that way in real life too. Do you see that?"

Brian: "Yeah…I guess I do. I never thought about it that way, but I do like how the game makes me feel. I want to feel that way in real life, and I guess that if I think of how good I am in the game, I can be that way in real life – somehow I feel more confident. I know that the bullies are only doing this because they see me as weak…"

Mom: "And do you see that if you live your life like you play the game that you won't appear weak? I mean, what if you carried the thought that you are one of the top players of this game in the world. How would things be different?"

Brian: "When you put it that way, I think I would walk around pretty confident. Oh, ok, I see what you are getting at now.

This dialogue revealed valuable information. First, Brian stated he would like to learn how to protect himself. For Brian's mother this was valuable information and she reassured him that she could make that happen for him. Second, Brian slowly began to see that the way the game made him feel was due to his ability to believe in himself and his confidence came from him demonstrating confidence and skill. By carrying this thought with him, Brian saw that he could transfer this confidence to any situation, and his confidence could not be shaken no matter who he was around or what circumstance he was experiencing. This is valuable for him because this can create a foundation upon which his social and emotional self can grow. Rather than continue in his cycle of isolation and despair, Brian now had a lighted path towards growth that helped him see the world in a more positive, strength-based way.

This case shows how powerful this approach can be, and I am here to tell you that any parent anywhere can learn this and put it into practice. Brian's mother, a single mom struggling to raise her son who lives with the challenges of AS/HFA, found a way to connect with him and learn ways to teach him and help him grow through a very difficult time of life. She carried a great deal of guilt and shame, thinking that she was "not enough" for Brian and believing he was "lost." Through making a commitment to connect with Brian, she realized she was enough; she was smarter than she thought she was, and she possessed a great deal of knowledge that she could teach him. There are a million cases like this all around the world, and I am inspired in my work to help these mothers and fathers see they are not failures and they are the greatest teachers and therapists their children will ever have. And it all begins with a commitment to connect on a deeper level.

A Word of Encouragement

While this case turned out well, some parents may find that their attempts at connection through video/computer games hit some snags. For example, one mother that I worked with was not allowed in the room where her son played his computer game! He was horrified that she wanted to enter "his private world." This was a huge barrier for her to overcome, but with persistence and a commitment to connection, she was able to overcome the barrier. I want to encourage you that if things do not go well, do not give up! Keep trying. Be imaginative and do not be afraid to keep trying; stay calm and let your heart guide you as you continue to seek a beautiful place of connection with your child.

Wii, XBOX 360 Kinect

The technology of today's video gaming systems allow for many new and innovative ways for whole families to get involved in game play. The Wii and XBOX 360 Kinect are two examples of gaming that allows physical activity to be combined with video technology. I find that many young people diagnosed with AS/HFA struggle with coordination of physical movement, and games that can be played on the Wii and XBOX 360 Kinect allow for these young people to practice movements that they normally would not perform. These games are also wonderful ways for parents to build connection with their children and adolescents and these games also provide opportunities for parents to cut loose and be goofy and silly, showing a side of themselves to their child that is fun and "outside the box." I encourage parents to take these opportunities when they come and use modern technology such as these games to build a deeper bond of connection with their child or adolescent.

Board Games

I wrote about board games in the section related to connecting with children, and I believe that it is important to include board games when discussing connecting with adolescents. Some parents are a bit shocked when I suggest connecting with their adolescent through a board game, but I find young people love board games no matter what their age. Board games have a great deal of practical usage for adolescents, particularly those diagnosed with AS/HFA. One is the games often have themes of connection and require social skills such as communication, turn-taking, and making decisions. I use board games in my group session with older adolescents diagnosed with AS/HFA for these reasons, and it helps them greatly in social situations to feel more competent and skilled in talking and sharing thoughts with others. Many individuals diagnosed with AS/HFA appear as though they do not understand a question and will stay silent for a number of seconds or even minutes following a question asked by a neurotypical individual. Most of us have been conditioned to respond to a question immediately or at least within a few seconds, which can actually get us into some trouble! Our culture moves quickly and demands that questions be answered immediately; however, many individuals diagnosed with AS/HFA view communication differently. Playing board games helps in the modeling of appropriate communication and social interaction, and gives young people a fun way to practice!

I learned about how individuals diagnosed with AS/HFA sometimes communicate differently the hard way and although I am embarrassed when I think of this valuable lesson, I want to share it with you because I think it is important. One young man that I worked with in my counseling office would take a long time to respond to questions. I use a lot of questions in my work, and I was inadvertently "firing" questions at this young man because I really wanted to know his thoughts about a particular topic. When he did not immediately respond, I would change the question and ask a slightly different question hoping that it would allow a quicker response. He stayed silent for a time, and then suddenly exploded in anger! He actually told me to "Stop!" He told me that his brain worked in a way that led him to analyze each question and go through every possible response before he answered my question. Obviously, the more questions I asked, the more responses he had to analyze. He shared with me that when I asked more and more questions it was like a log jam in his mind, and the more logs there were, the more work it took to be done to get rid of the logs. He suddenly found himself overwhelmed and at a loss of what to do with all the questions and possible responses. In addition, he shared with me that he not only analyzed his responses but that he would attempt to predict the response of the individual as well; this process obviously took a great deal of time and emotional and mental energy. He shared with me when he attempted to engage in conversation with people in the "real world" and things did not go well, he would simply shut down and walk away, leaving the person asking the questions confused or hurt. Suddenly, I realized the typical way that neurotypical individuals engage in conversation was completely different to how many individuals diagnosed with AS/HFA communicate. Like this young man, many individuals diagnosed with AS/HFA that I meet tend to dissect information and are very detailed in examining that information and in formulating a verbal response. I am so grateful this young man got angry and let me know how his brain worked! I was humbled, but also learned a lot that day. I realized when this young man did respond, his response was detailed and offered valuable information. After apologizing profusely, I shared with this young man that if he could "speed up" the process, his conversations may go better and I explained to him how a neurotypical brain worked and how our culture forces us to give quick responses, and sometimes this gets people in trouble. I praised him for his practice of taking time to respond, but also pointed out that neurotypical individuals may interpret this as being rude or ignorant.

I used several board games with him in our individual work as well as in group to help him get better at giving a quicker response. This helped him in a fun and less intrusive way. Games such as "Outburst," "Catch Phrase," and "Sorry" are a few examples of games that have elements of making quick decisions and communicating responses in a quick manner. Over time, this young man was able to analyze information from questions more quickly and realized he did not have to analyze every possible response; he found he could isolate only the information needed to answer the question. He grasped the idea of how he was wasting a lot of energy trying to predict the response of the other person, and was relieved to know he did not have to do this. This realization reduced a great deal of pressure for this young man, and made social interaction with others much easier. This is an example of how board games can be very helpful in helping a young person diagnosed with AS/HFA practice valuable social skills.

Another positive that comes from playing a board game with an adolescent diagnosed with AS/HFA is that it creates deeper connection through opening up channels of dialogue. Most board games require communication; can you imagine playing a game of LIFE and not speaking throughout the entire game? I encourage parents that simply creating the opportunity for connection through a board game can bring about good communication on two levels. One level is the "simple" dialogue related to setting up the game and playing it; the other level is a deeper communication related to making decisions about career, money, marriage, and children. For example, one family that I worked with used the game of LIFE to build greater connection with their young person diagnosed with AS/HFA and his neurotypical siblings. These parents shared with me that they were unaware of their son's thoughts about career, marriage, and college until they sat down to play LIFE. They were also pleasantly surprised to see a range of emotion in their son as a result of the game play. Emotions such as elation and excitement were something they had not seen in some time. Another positive was this young man engaged in communication with his siblings as a result of playing the game. I love sharing with parents and families how board games are more than just "games;" these games provide opportunities for connection, communication, and help the young person think about his or her future.

Games such as LIFE and Monopoly also provide the opportunity for the young person to practice handling money and thinking about the price of things. One of the challenges in our culture is teaching our young people the value of hard work, and how money is something that must be earned. Most of us live in prosperity when compared with the rest of the world, and it is our duty to teach our children the value of money and making wise decisions about spending that money. Board games are a fun way to open up dialogue about such matters. I find adolescents diagnosed with AS/HFA are usually terrified to think of living on their own, and those who think they are ready usually do not understand all that independence entails.

Through playing board games which contain themes of preparing for independence, parents have a great tool to begin helping young people think about what it takes to live on their own.

A third positive that comes from playing a board game with an adolescent diagnosed with AS/HFA is the opportunity to help them learn to manage emotions. Games in general can elicit a great deal of emotion, from elation and surprise, to devastation and disappointment. I have witnessed a great deal of emotion during board game play in my years of individual and group with young people diagnosed with AS/HFA. One vivid memory that I have is that one young man's obsession to keep the UNO cards completely straight after each play (he straightened the pile every time someone laid down a card) caused another young man to throw his cards in anger and refuse to play because of how the game was slowed to a crawl as a result of the obsessive behavior. I remained calm and used the incident to talk about the various emotions that each member was feeling (anger, fear, frustration, etc.) and used the incident as a learning opportunity for all involved and teaching them how to feel the emotion but to learn not to react. I have witnessed younger children diagnosed with AS/HFA break down in tears when they did not land on their favorite space in the game or did not win – another golden opportunity to comfort them and help them understand what they are feeling and to learn to get through the experience.

How to Help Your Child/Adolescent when Emotions Surface

Regardless of what type of game you are playing, whether electronic or board game, emotions are likely to surface. Parents are often caught off guard by their child's emotional reaction, whether the child is diagnosed with AS/HFA or not, and most of us are not prepared to deal with the situation because when we sense that our children are not "okay" our "fight-or-flight" response triggers. Parents usually respond in one of three ways: Over-protective reactive response ("We'll just throw that bike away! It hurt you didn't it?"); Anger reaction ("Stop crying or I'll give you something to cry about"); or completely ignoring the child's emotional release altogether which sends the message to the child that the parent is unavailable to assist the child when the child is emotionally overwhelmed. No parent wants to see his or her child sad or upset; however, I teach parents in my parenting classes that allowing a child to be sad is very important. When parents "rush in" to stop a child's sadness either by telling them that they "shouldn't" be sad or buy them things to instantly soothe them, that child begins to believe that he should never be sad and if he is sad, that there is something wrong with him and that the sadness must be eradicated at all costs. As the child develops, she may never develop the skills necessary to tolerate unpleasant emotions, which can cause many problems in forming and sustaining relationships and may lead to addiction issues as substances of all forms are used to "soothe" emotional pain.

Individuals diagnosed with AS/HFA tend to struggle with understanding their own emotions and the emotions of others (alexithymia) and parents play an even more important role in helping these children or adolescents navigate these waters. I will discuss this further in the next chapter when I discuss consequences, but I want to share a few quick tips on helping your child or adolescent learn to understand and manage emotions when they surface during game play.

1. *Maintain a non-reactive presence.* Relax your stomach and maintain a demeanor of calmness and safety.
2. *Speak in a calm, steady voice.* Change in tone or pitch can be triggers, and many individuals diagnosed with AS/HFA are sensitive to voice tone. Keep your volume at a steady, even level and be mindful of how you sound.
3. *Make eye contact and remind the child or adolescent that he or she is safe and in a safe place.* Remind the child or adolescent that you are there with him and that there is no one there that is going to hurt him.
4. *Encourage the young person to put her thoughts and feelings into words.* You may need to use prompts, such as "Tell me what you are feeling;" or "Tell me what you are thinking right now."
5. *Remind siblings that only words of kindness and love are needed at this time, and they are free to leave the room if they cannot be encouraging and supportive.* Sometimes siblings use the emotional outburst of their sibling diagnosed with AS/HFA as leverage to make themselves feel better and to "dominate" the sibling. This is not because they are mean-spirited or seek to do irreparable damage; it is simply what emotionally immature individuals do, and siblings (especially younger ones) often lack the maturity to handle their own emotions. However, parents need to enforce the importance of family and the home is a place of love and safety. I encourage parents to enforce this with both the individual diagnosed with AS/HFA as well as with neurotypical siblings.

6. *Do your best to work through the emotional outburst and get back to the game.* It is important for everyone involved to be able to weather the emotional storm and return to the game; however, it may not be possible. It may be best to allow a "cool down" period. I encourage parents to use their best judgment. If it is not possible to return to the game, make sure that the incident is not ignored, but that it is processed with each family member involved. This can be done by meeting individually with each family member in private or by having a family meeting (more on that in the next chapter!). Remember that the goal when dealing with emotional outbursts is that each person involved (especially the individual diagnosed with AS/HFA) learns something from the experience.

Music/Movies/TV Shows

Another great way to connect with an adolescent diagnosed with AS/HFA is to use music, movies, or a TV show the young person enjoys as a way to better understand how the young person thinks and feels. I do this often in my work with young people diagnosed with AS/HFA because they often struggle with communicating their thoughts and feelings, and many find it easier to relate to a show or song. I look for the themes that are present in a particular song or movie and find these themes often reveal what the young person is thinking or feeling. I find young people are usually excited to know I want to watch what they watch and listen to what they listen to, and communication is opened between us. I share with parents this can be a vehicle towards better understand their young person and creating greater connection with their adolescent diagnosed with AS/HFA.

More Than Just a "Kid's Show"

One of the most amazing experiences that I have had in my work happened with a young man who struggled with communicating his thoughts and feelings with me and others. Like many individuals diagnosed with AS/HFA, he was very intelligent and his brain worked at such a high level that he micromanaged every thought he had, which made communication very difficult because even a simple conversation took a long time while I waited for him to sift through every piece of a question that I asked or comment that I made. One day he asked me if he could bring in a DVD of a show that he really liked, and I said "yes." I always allow young people to bring in movies, music, or TV show clips that mean a lot to them because I have found these can be a window to a young person's soul and are especially useful in working with those diagnosed with AS/HFA. The show the young man brought to me was an animated series that ran for three seasons. Because there were no commercials, each episode was about twenty-five minutes and then we would take the rest of the session to discuss his thoughts and feelings about the characters or the plot of the show. I was amazed as we began watching the show how animated he became and excited as he talked about the show. He was more verbal and using his hands as he stopped the DVD from time to time to tell me about the background of the story. To my surprise, he picked up on the subtle humor embedded in the show, something that I had not witnessed prior to watching the show with him. I was instantly drawn to several themes in the show that proved to be applicable to my work with this young man, themes such as loyalty, determination, working with others to solve problems, believing in oneself, and dealing with discouragement. I became excited as I realized how I could use something that he was passionate about in the therapy process. I noticed he was excited that I was truly interested in the show, and I made sure I thanked him and assured him that we could watch them during each session. Over the course of the next six months, I was amazed, entertained, and thrilled about this show that on the surface appeared to be a "kid's show." As we watched this show, this young man came alive and as I used the metaphors from the show to help show him not to be afraid of the future and to help him learn to connect with others in new ways. Perhaps the greatest element that I took from the show was the theme of establishing safety for this young man and helping him gain more self-confidence through teaching him ways to self-soothe when he was in a situation that was unfamiliar to him or around people that he did not know.

The Most Unlikely Rap Fan

I worked with a young man diagnosed with AS/HFA and used his love of rap music to help him learn to put thoughts and feelings into words. I have written earlier in the book about how individuals diagnosed with AS/HFA often struggle with putting thoughts and feelings into words and this was very difficult for this young man. When I began working with him, it was difficult to get him to speak, and he appeared uneasy. I spent a great amount of time finding out what he enjoyed, and one day I pulled up YouTube on my computer and asked him what he would like to see. He stared at me blankly and I waited for his response. "I like rap music" he said quietly. "Rap music" I said, "Ok, what is your favorite song or artist?" He shyly told me that he liked Eminem and Notorious B.I.G. and told me some of the songs that he liked by both artists. I began to search the songs and bring them up for us to watch. I must admit that I did not listen to rap music on a regular basis, but this young man gave me quite an education. I began to see rap as a powerful form of poetry and narrative of difficult experiences; the everyday struggle of humanity dealing with loss, poverty, oppression, and relationships. I pulled themes from the songs such as anger, frustration, loss, survival, and the struggle of getting through the day. Much like the young man in the previous case, this young man became animated as he talked about the songs he liked and the content of the lyrics. He could recite the lyrics by heart and when he recited them I noticed passion and his voice followed the exact cadence and rhythm of the rappers. We dissected the songs and he was able to tell me why he liked certain songs and I used the emotions that he experienced as a way to help him learn to put the feelings into words. There was a metaphor with how he felt in the "real world" in social situations that connected to the themes of survival and struggle in the songs; there was a connection to the feelings of rage and rejection in the songs that he related to when he was bullied and rejected by peers. We were also able to find appropriate outlets for his anger such as writing his own raps and rapping them instead of "stuffing" it. As a result of our work together, this young man improved in being able to understand emotions, communicating his thoughts and feelings to others, and learning how to manage his emotions instead of turning them inward.

A Final Word to Parents

These two cases demonstrate how powerful it is to connect with adolescents through a favorite movie, music they love, or TV show they enjoy. For parents of adolescents diagnosed with AS/HFA, these mediums provide powerful paths to connection and windows to the young person's heart. These mediums can foster greater chances for increased communication between the young person and parents, and also provide the parent with tools to teach the young person valuable social skills and tools he or she will need for independent living through the themes found in these mediums. Remember the power of patience, setting aside previously held judgments regarding a TV show or type of music, and placing connection at the forefront of your mind. Remember the power of "just be." Strive to be like an explorer in a new land, looking for rare gems and being curious about all that you will find. I am convinced that you will be amazed, much like I am each day as I spend time with these amazing young people.

CHAPTER 7

Discipline and Correction: Building and Sustaining Connection through the Application of Age-Appropriate Consequences for Poor Choices and Negative Behavior

The Great Discipline Dilemma for Parents/Caregivers

Many families with whom I work struggle in discerning if the negative behavior of their child or adolescent is willful disobedience that requires discipline or if it is simply "Asperger stuff." "Asperger stuff" is the quirks and behaviors that are part of the child or adolescent's behavioral repertoire and are not necessarily purposeful attempts to hurt another person or intended to be selfish in nature. However, the behavior of these young people can create a great deal of chaos and their behavioral choices can be hurtful to those around them and can be interpreted as mean-spirited and vindictive. I often hear stories of "ruined" vacations, restaurant trips that are "disastrous" and other family functions that end up in family members being frustrated and in tears. While many parents understand that it is hard for their young person diagnosed with AS/HFA to see things from other's perspectives and the young person struggles with understanding his or her emotions and the emotional reactions of others, the parents still feel something must be done about the way their child or adolescent treats them or other family members. I want to help you get through these dilemmas and to provide you with guidance that will help calm these rough waters. A full discussion of parenting strategies is beyond the scope of this book; however, I have included an appendix with a list of books that provide help with discipline and handling behavioral and emotional outbursts. In this chapter, I will discuss the various factors that make discipline situations difficult and how to differentiate between behavior that is part of the landscape of AS/HFA and what is not. Most importantly, I will share effective ways to handle these difficult situations while maintaining connection with your child or adolescent diagnosed with AS/HFA in order to maintain family connection as well.

Factors that Make Discipline Difficult

CHARACTERISTICS OF AS/HFA

A factor making the area of discipline difficult is simply the characteristics of AS/HFA. Mindblindness and alexithymia are two of the major factors that create confusion for the young person diagnosed with AS/HFA when parents and other authority figures attempt to enforce discipline for undesired behavior. The purpose of consequences and discipline is to teach. The authority figure attempts to apply a consequence to teach the young person that the chosen behavior is not appropriate and a better choice is needed the next time the situation arises. For learning to occur, the young person must be able to see the situation from multiple perspectives. Children and adolescents diagnosed with AS/HFA tend to only see situations from one perspective, and it is almost as if they have "tunnel vision." Nearly all children, whether diagnosed with AS/HFA or not, tend to try to "wiggle" out of trouble and often refuse to take responsibility when being disciplined for poor choices. However, with consistent and firm boundaries applied by the parent, most children and adolescents "get it" and realize that the key to their freedom lies in making good choices. Children and adolescents diagnosed with AS/HFA can often interpret attempts by parents and other authority figures to apply consequences as a concerted effort to make their lives miserable and I often hear young people say they think their parents "hate" them when the parent takes away a privilege or gives the young person an extra chore because of poor choices the young person has made.

I worked with a young man of about fifteen who was diagnosed with AS/HFA and I was helping his parents find appropriate consequences for undesired behavior. I helped his parents devise a clear and simple consequence list for poor choices and we reviewed it together in one of the sessions. While going over the list, the young man snorted and mumbled under his breath and appeared thoroughly annoyed. During the last half of the session, I met with him individually to help get him to see this discipline plan came from his parent's love for him and that if he made good choices, he actually could actually earn the things he so desperately wanted. I also tried to get him to see this plan was a vast improvement from the way his parents were previously handling discipline and consequences, which was inconsistent and vacillated from extreme to non-existent. He wanted to hear none of that, however. He shared with me this was a clear attempt to take away his freedom and because his parents thought he was "stupid" and he believed they wanted him to be miserable.

No matter what I said, and no matter how I said it, this young man could not see things from a perspective other than what he believed. I brought up several instances where his parents had shown great leniency and had given him multiple chances but he just stared at me with a blank stare. "This is the dumbest thing I have ever heard," he snorted.

I must admit it was very frustrating to not be able to help this young man see things from another perspective. The good news is the parents implemented the rewards/consequences plan we devised and it worked very well, and the young man responded positively. After conversations such as this, I spend a great deal of time thinking about what life is like for the young people that I interact with from day to day. I often take longs walks in the evenings and think about my sessions with the various children and adolescents diagnosed with AS/HFA and their families. I thought about this young man and wondered what it was like to be him, and how confusing it must be to encounter situations like this at home, at school, and with peers. I thought about how frustrating it would be to exist in a world where people rarely saw things "my way." I also thought about how it would be to think the structure and order that my parents were trying to implement was to hurt me and make my life miserable. I felt a surge of empathy for this young man, and I realized after doing this he was not trying to be difficult and he was not purposely lashing out at his parents because he was "a selfish brat," as many of these young people are labeled. No, it was because he literally could not see things from a different perspective, and even though he followed the rules his parents set and reaped the benefits from making good choices, he probably would never change his opinion.

Alexithymia, the inability to understand one's own emotions or the emotions of others, also causes difficulties for a young person diagnosed with AS/HFA to understand what is going on when a parent or authority figure attempts to provide consequences for undesired behavior. I remind parents that when emotions are involved with any child or adolescent, logic and reasoning goes out the window. For young people diagnosed with AS/HFA, emotional eruptions can be like tropical storms that seemingly come out of nowhere and may last from a few minutes to hours. Mindblindness and alexithymia tend to go hand in hand because when young people are unable to see something from a different perspective, as in the case of the young man above, negative emotions such as frustration and anger can arise and further disrupt the process. Again, this is why I stress to parents to stay non-reactive and present a calm and firm front to the young person. When the young person is "triggered" and is in a negative emotional state, logic and reasoning are disrupted and learning cannot take place. It is normal for young people diagnosed with AS/HFA to respond negatively to consequences for undesired behavior and display tantrum behavior. However, when the parent models firmness, a calm demeanor, and holds the young person responsible for making good choices, there is a greater chance that the young person will understand what is happening. The good news is that these emotional storms diminish and through a parent being consistent, calm, and firm, the behavior of the young person is gradually shaped and molded towards more positive and socially acceptable forms.

"But My Child has Special Needs"

Another factor making discipline difficult is the attitude of the parent or caregiver that because of the child or adolescent's "special needs" related to the diagnosis of AS/HFA, parents feel it would be "cruel" or "unfair" to hold these children to a system of consequences or discipline. The end result of this thinking is that a child or adolescent grows into an adult expecting favored treatment and the belief that she should get whatever she wants when she wants it. Parents of children who have special needs as a result of a disability often battle this type of thinking, and often feel like the child has to endure so much that the parent(s) do not relish the idea of applying consequences for poor behavior. These parents are also afraid of the emotional reaction of the child. When the child or adolescent is upset, these parents tend to blame themselves and I find these parents carry a great deal of guilt. Parents in these scenarios often excuse the behavior of the young person with special needs and understandably have a hard time when it comes time to discipline their child for negative behavior. Please understand I am empathic towards these families and in no way am I judging them in an accusatory manner. I am simply bringing to light the fact that while having a child or adolescent diagnosed with AS/HFA is a challenge, these young people still need firm boundaries and consequences for poor behavioral choices to help them learn and be as independent as possible.

I work hard to help parents shed this belief because I believe neglecting to provide firm consequences for poor behavior choices for children or adolescents is akin to giving them a gun to play with or buying drugs and alcohol for them to consume. While children and adolescents diagnosed with AS/HFA need to be given some consideration for their challenges and difficulties, maintaining firm and consistent boundaries are necessary to help them learn to make good choices and become better problem solvers. Social situations are often difficult for young people diagnosed with AS/HFA because they require both emotional control and the cognitive ability to think through situations. By providing a firm and consistent system of consequences for poor behavioral choices and rewards for positive behavioral choices, the young person is able to learn these valuable skills, even though they might not agree with them or completely understand them. I have worked with several young people diagnosed with AS/HFA who have transitioned from adolescence into adulthood and have shared with me that while they do not always understand why certain social situations call for certain social behavior, they know it is simply "the social rules" and the rules must be followed or there will be consequences. I remind parents that the earlier they begin a solid pattern of rewards and consequences, the better it is for the young person as well as for the parents and the family.

"I DON'T KNOW WHAT BEHAVIOR NEEDS TO BE DISCIPLINED AND WHAT BEHAVIOR SHOULDN'T"

I hear this from parents often, and my heart goes out to them. If parents of children and adolescents diagnosed with AS/HFA attempted to discipline *every* negative behavior many would constantly feel like a jail warden and their child or adolescent would probably feel completely overwhelmed on a constant basis. Obviously, some behaviors need to be overlooked but which ones should be ignored and which should have consequences applied to them? Professionals who work with children know ignoring certain negative behaviors can often help extinguish those behaviors; however, they also know this does not always work and the behaviors may become more frequent, especially when there are extenuating circumstances such as the challenges that AS/HFA can bring. Ignoring certain behaviors can appear to a child or adolescent that the adult is giving approval to those behaviors, and for children and adolescents diagnosed with AS/HFA who tend to be confused by social rules in the first place, they may further misconstrue the adults' ignoring of the behavior as silent approval. Many parents often are inconsistent because of this, coming down too harshly over some behavioral choices and completely ignoring others, especially when they are tired or too distracted to properly deal with the negative behaviors.

I have discovered an easier way to solve this dilemma. I share this solution with parents and encourage them to use a simple guide that eases the burden of trying to decide what behavior should be disciplined and what behavior should be ignored. The first thing I share with parents is to know their child through and through.

What I mean by this is that parents should know their child or adolescent's pattern of behavior and what triggers them. I remind parents often that their child is not in a book or on a website, and there is not a professional alive who knows their child better than the parents, who have spent every day with their child. I challenge parents to make a list of the common triggers that "set off" their child, the situations that contain these triggers, and the common emotional reactions that their child exhibits. For example, perhaps the negative behavior occurs when the child or adolescent is fatigued, and occurs at the end of the day after a full day of school. The behavior may occur when the child reacts to something out of the ordinary routine the child is used to. It is important to know these things because it helps narrow down what may be a reasonable reaction for the child and what is not, given the stressor.

The second step is similar to the first but it involves parents examining which parts of their child or adolescent's behavior is manipulative or something the child does to get what he or she wants after the parent has said "no." (Please do not think I am encouraging you to see your child in a negative light; I am simply teaching you to learn all there is about your child or adolescent). It is common for young people to go through phases where they may lie or seek to manipulate others to get what they want, and a positive way to look at this is that the child or adolescent is doing what she thinks she has to do to make herself feel safe. It is frightening for children or adolescents to take responsibility for a wrong choice because they often do not have the emotional maturity required to accept blame and take corrective action. The parent should identify the patterns of behavior that constitute this manipulative type of behavior. Again, this is not to punish the child or use this against him; it is simply to help the parent see that the child attempts to be in control as a way to help him feel safe. The child may also use the manipulative behavior as a way to gain attention. This step of evaluating if the behavior of the child is an attempt to manipulate the parent is helpful because it makes the parent a wise behavioral analyst and also helps the parent become resilient to the manipulative efforts of the child or adolescent.

The third step in this process is similar to both step one and two and involves the parent knowing the "quirks" of their child or adolescent diagnosed with AS/HFA. What I mean by this is all young people diagnosed with AS/HFA have a unique characteristic that sets them apart, "quirks" that are simply a behavior or behaviors these young people exhibit making them who they are. It might be the young person counts when he gets nervous; it may be a tic like a body movement or a phrase that the child says repeatedly. This may also be something that the child likes to do or perhaps it is a toy or object that she likes to have to provide her comfort or joy. The reason quirks are important is because the parents need to have a thorough understanding of their child or adolescent to be as prepared as possible to ascertain what behavior can be ignored and dismissed as part of the AS/HFA landscape, and what behavior is manipulative or "negative" and needs to be shaped through the application of consequences.

The fourth step relates to the concept of teaching through shaping and molding behavior through the application of consequences. The parent should ascertain if the behavior of the child is a pattern or a behavior which occurs repeatedly and on a regular basis and if that behavior is socially unacceptable. A socially unacceptable behavior is a behavior that would cause a disruption in a relationship or a social setting that most people would find inappropriate. If the answer is "yes" to the behavior, then the parent needs to apply consequences for the specified behavior in order to teach the young person appropriate behavior. Note that I said that the behavior is a pattern or a behavior that is repeated. This is important because as I said earlier, children and adolescents diagnosed with AS/HFA often display socially inappropriate behaviors now and then and we must remember that it is not because they mean to, but simply because they, like any other child or adolescent, is learning socially appropriate behavior as well as dealing with all of the challenges AS/HFA brings. It is understandable there will be a behavioral "hiccup" now and then. What the parent must look for is the pattern and repeated behaviors that need to be gradually changed. Behaviors like outbursts, tantrums, lack of hygiene, disrespect, and use of inappropriate words and phrases occurring on a regular basis are examples of behaviors for which consequences should be given.

From these four elements, parents should make a short checklist that they can keep in mind that to help when a behavioral dilemma arises. It looks like this:

1. Has something triggered my child or adolescent that is causing this behavior? (Is he tired, hungry, or out of routine).
2. Is this behavior because my child or adolescent desires attention or is trying to be in control? (Is she feeling unsafe or needing reassurance?)
3. Is this behavior simply a "quirk" that is part of my child or adolescent's behavioral repertoire? (Something that is part of who he is and something that I can ignore?)
4. Is this behavior socially unacceptable and occurs repeatedly on a regular basis and causes disruption in relationship?

This checklist provides a parent with a guide that can help them decide if consequences are needed or if the behavior can be ignored. I also want to point out that using a checklist such as this forces the parents to stay grounded to the moment and use logic and stay rational, which helps to keep the parent out of "fight or flight" mode. Let us look at a few case examples to see how this would work.

Case Example Number One: James

Imagine James, young boy diagnosed with AS/HFA is acting out negatively while waiting with his mother in the check-out line at the grocery store. James is whining and flailing around because he notices his favorite candy bar in the checkout line and he wants the candy bar. His mother Jill has told him it is too close to dinner for him to get a candy bar and they will be home soon. While Jill is not happy about the behavior, she quickly does a mental rundown of the above list and realizes James is hungry and she had to run an extra errand after picking him up from school, which was outside the normal routine (Checkmark on Number One). Jill also remembers what her counselor shared with her about the brain and how many young people on the autism spectrum act out because of a need to feel safe, and she realizes because of her son feeling unsafe (out of routine, tired, and hungry) he is looking to the candy bar to bring him a sense of safety (Checkmark on Number Two). Jill thinks about how this particular brand of candy bar is James' absolute favorite thing to eat and often receives the privilege of getting the candy bar as a reward for appropriate behavior (Checkmark on Number Three). Jill reviews his current behavior and realizes because of the "hits" on one, two and three above, his behavior is actually normal and quite typical of most children in these situations, not to mention those diagnosed with AS/HFA. She decides to ignore James' behavior and firmly but quietly reminds him he can earn extra video game time this evening if he can help her carry the bags to the car. She reassures him they will eat as soon as they get home. His whining does not cease but immediately becomes quieter. Jill then adopts a "business as usual" mindset and moves through the checkout process with no more words to her son, and soon the two of them are moving out the door of the grocery store towards the car.

Discussion of Case Number One.   Notice Jill quickly went down the checklist and was able to immediately see the situation from a different perspective. When parents becomes triggered by their child's behaviors and responds in a negative emotional manner, it is usually because the parent is viewing the situation from their perspective only (which, interestingly, is why the child is acting out). The decision to either not deal with the negative behavior, or come down on the young person too harshly, is rooted in the selfish desires of the parent to either ignore it ("I will be embarrassed if I address the behavior") or come down extremely harshly ("Others will think I'm a "bad" mother if I don't save face") which often results in yelling or sometimes, sadly, hitting the child. This mother stayed in "logic and reasoning" mode and while she felt emotionally aroused, she did not act on the emotions of anger, frustration, or embarrassment. Note also the behavior of James did not magically go away either; in fact, he continued to whine, although the volume of the whining did go down a notch. I remind parents sometimes things will get worse for a time when the parent first implements these steps and it is simply a matter of conditioning. If the child is used to being able to get his or her way through acting out in a negative way, then it makes sense the child is going to "ramp-up" the acting out until he or she realize the parent is the "wall of China" and not going to give in. Jill, in this situation, exhibited patience, stayed calm, and was non-reactive and appeared confident and competent, which helped her model appropriate behavior for her son in a social situation in which he was feeling unsafe and uncomfortable. She also reassured him they would eat as soon as they got home.

CASE EXAMPLE NUMBER TWO: MOLLY

Imagine Molly, a young girl diagnosed with AS/HFA who is refusing to do her homework because she wants to play her favorite video game. Her parents, Tom and Diane, have put in place a solid rule about homework: Those who want to play their video games will complete their homework. While Molly is very intelligent, she does not like the "work" part of her math homework and this is a common power struggle each evening. She is yelling and crying, and demonstrating her resistance by shoving her papers off the kitchen table. Tom and Diane do a quick evaluation using the checklist and they determine there is nothing that has triggered their daughter other than the situation involving the math homework she does not want to do. There has been no disruption in routine and their daughter is not hungry or tired from any noticeable trigger (No checkmark on Number One). Moving down the list, Tom and Diane determine she is indeed reacting out of a need to be in control which has resulted in a classic power struggle ("I don't want to do my math home-work"); however, they realize this negative reaction stems from her not feeling safe in this situation and Molly is doing all she can to get away from the threat (math homework) (Checkmark on Number Two). I point this out because many parents are conditioned to see their children as "bad" or "defiant" when a situation like this occurs; I remind parents this is a "fight or flight" phenomenon and calls for the parent to be calm, non-reactive, and in control so the parent can think through the situation. Moving down the list, Tom and Diane remind themselves this is familiar territory with their daughter: She hates math homework and more importantly, when she encounters a situation in which she feels overwhelmed, she often will become aggressive and act out in a negative manner with yelling, crying, or physically pushing them away (Checkmark on Number Three). Tom and Diane remind each other to relax their stomachs and ground themselves to the moment, and instead of one or both becoming angry and hostile to each other or to Molly, they bond as partners and teammates and show Molly a united front. Tom and Diane find they must put a checkmark on Number Four, and determine Molly's behavior is indeed socially unacceptable and definitely needs a consequence because it occurs on a regular basis. They review their options of immediate consequences which include removing her from the situation and putting her in time out, taking away the video game privilege for the evening, or taking the game away but letting her earn the privilege back if she can calm down in a reasonable amount of time. They also would like her to learn to ask for help instead of instantly becoming violent and out of control emotionally, so the parents have begun adding this to the list of appropriate responses. They have also learned some behavioral techniques of shortening math homework time to short sequences of work, such as ten minute increments with breaks in between and the parents have added this to their toolbox. However, in this situation, her behavior is escalating and the parents recognize she is "ramping up" and soon her ability to listen to logic or reasoning will be completely shut off.

Diane takes the lead and calmly and firmly tells Molly that she has choices: She can take a break and go to her room to calm down, or she can ask for help from Mom or Dad, but the math homework must be done before she can play her video game. If she continues, she will not be able to play the game that night. Diane asks Molly, "Do you understand?" and seeks to connect with Molly's eyes as she asks this. Diane is careful to communicate love, patience, and tenderness and in a brief second Molly's eyes connect with Diane's and suddenly a softening occurs. Molly continues to cry, but she is no longer flailing or wailing. "Help me understand what you want," Diane asks gently. Through deep breaths and sobs, Molly says softly, "I need help with it...I feel like I can't do it," and then begins a new round of sobs and collapses into Diane's chest and Diane holds her and says, "It's ok to cry. You are safe here! Please cry if you want to." After several minutes, the crying ceases and Tom helps Molly with the math homework which is completed in about twenty minutes. Molly gets to play her video game because she chose to finish her homework.

Discussion of Case Number Two. Notice at no point in this scenario did Tom or Diane raise their voice or use threats to redirect Molly. They stayed calm, even though Molly's behavior was "ramping up." While they were ready to implement consequences if they needed to, they never stopped trying to connect with Molly. Had Molly not calmed down, Tom would have said firmly, "Molly, your behavior is inappropriate. Would you like to walk to your room on your own or would you like me to help you get there?" Notice also Diane used her eye contact not to intimidate or display anger, but to communicate tenderness, love, and sincerity. Even in the midst of this emotional and behavioral "hurricane," Tom and Diane never stopped communicating a message of safety and connection. I remind parents often, whether they have a child on the autism spectrum or not, children "feed" off the emotional and physical presence of their parents. While a parent remaining calm does not guarantee a child will never act out, it has a big influence on the intensity and duration of the episode. From a conditioning standpoint, a parent's reaction impacts what the child expects from mom or dad. This means if parents often respond in a volatile manner, or if they are unpredictable (calm sometimes, but sometimes yelling), the child is more likely to not know how the parent will respond and the child or adolescent is likely to act out intensely because he or she is not sure what to expect from mom or dad and this keeps them in "fight or flight" mode. When parents are consistent and firm just like Tom and Diane were in this situation, the child is likely to be able to self-soothe on her own and respond to prompts because the child understands the parent's love is unconditional and the child has the freedom to make better choices.

"How do I Discipline my Child with Asperger's when I have Neurotypical Children?"

A major difficulty for parents of young people diagnosed with AS/HFA is when there are neurotypical siblings in the family dynamic which results in the parents trying to balance a system of rewards/consequences for the child or adolescent diagnosed with AS/HFA and a system of rewards/consequences for the neurotypical sibling. Many parents I meet in my practice often report this problem as their most difficult and it causes a great deal of strife within the home. I have conducted family sessions and heard from neurotypical siblings who feel their parents "baby" the sibling diagnosed with AS/HFA and there is a second set of standards for their special needs sibling. I witness a great deal of anger, hostility, and resentment from these siblings, which often results in the siblings rejecting their sibling diagnosed with AS/HFA or ganging up on him or her through aligning with other family members. The parent or parents in these situations report they feel lost and "caught in the middle" when these situations arise. The parents knows if they allow certain behaviors for their child diagnosed with AS/HFA and not the neurotypical siblings, the other siblings will notice and want the same "breaks;" and if the parents hold the child diagnosed with AS/HFA to the same standards as their siblings, the child may feel overwhelmed if those standards are too high for them. So what is a parent to do to resolve this dilemma? Thankfully, there is a solution and I believe it is one that works for everyone involved and also serves to build connection within the family. The solution involves three principles.

First, the sibling or siblings should know about the differences of their brother or sister diagnosed with AS/HFA. This is not to make the child or adolescent diagnosed with AS/HFA a "victim" or to demand they get special treatment, or to humiliate them, but as a way of informing the siblings so they are educated and aware of the challenges. The purpose of this education is to promote understanding and connection. When neurotypical siblings understand why their sibling diagnosed with AS/HFA may appear "odd" or react in a non-typical manner, it can help the siblings be more patient and the siblings will be less likely to lash out at or reject the young person diagnosed with AS/HFA. From a positive perspective, the siblings can also learn to appreciate the special talents and gifts of the young person diagnosed with AS/HFA, which fosters connection instead of competition. This principle lays a foundation from which the parents can formulate a foundation of rewards/consequences based on fairness and understanding for all involved.

The second principle is that the parents have a clear and consistent program for rewards/consequences for all their children both neurotypical and those diagnosed with AS/HFA. A successful company has a policy and procedure manual and so does a successful family. A successful sports program has a coaching staff that has a plan and a way to implement the plan, and parenting children should run in the same manner. Most parents run into difficulties regarding discipline because they are always reacting to their children's behavior and attempting to dole out consequences as they happen and the parents either come down extremely harshly ("You are grounded from the XBOX for the whole school year") or in an inconsistent manner (sometimes applying discipline and sometimes not). Imagine a coaching staff whose philosophy is, "We'll wait until we see what happens out there on the field and then figure it out." This would probably not work very well, so why do parents approach parenting in this manner? For parents trying to navigate the waters of parenting with a child or adolescent diagnosed with AS/HFA and neurotypical siblings they need to have a "playbook" that is a clear and consistent approach to dealing with negative behaviors, and should be the same across the board for all of the young people in the home. The parents will need to make accommodations and changes based on the situation and also the characteristics of the child (this is true of parenting regardless of whether the child is diagnosed with AS/HFA or not); however, their children will know what to expect when they make negative choices and the parents will not be caught off guard. Thus, the parent operates in a proactive rather than reactive manner.

The third principle relates to the parents being firm and consistent in all situations involving a child's negative behavior, whether neurotypical or diagnosed with AS/HFA. This also means that parents do not argue with, negotiate, or explain themselves to a child when applying a consequence, nor do parents explain themselves to a neurotypical sibling who is trying to criticize the parent's decision to either apply consequences or ignore a negative behavior. Too often in my office I encounter parents who make problems for themselves because they attempt to explain their parenting decisions to siblings who are being critical of their approach. I instruct them to firmly remind their children or adolescents that it is not their problem, and if they continue to attempt to intervene, they will receive a consequence. While this may seem harsh, it sends the message to all involved that the parents are in control and the young person is not needed in the discipline of a sibling or siblings. I always remind parents this should be done calmly and without yelling or losing control of themselves emotionally. Be firm, be clear, and speak in a calm and controlled voice.

These three principles are valuable because they take away the dynamic of the parent trying to discipline their child or adolescent diagnosed with AS/HFA in one way and applying a different set of expectations for their neurotypical children. Children are bright and are sensitive to unfairness and they almost automatically notice when a differing set of standards is being used. Certainly, this is a very difficult dilemma for families with a child or adolescent diagnosed with AS/HFA in the mix. With this dilemma removed, the parents can present a solid front of the same expectations for all their children across all situations. Wise parents always keep in mind that they carry "veto" power and have the ability to modify consequences based on the circumstances, and I remind parents to not be afraid to use this power when the need arises. At the right time, (which I will discuss later in this chapter) a parent can discuss it with the other family members to explain the reasoning for their parenting decisions, but never attempt this in the heat of the moment. Simply re-direct the siblings towards a positive activity that is away from the situation or remind them that they can be most helpful by being silent and you will address the issue with them at a later time.

"I'm a Single Parent and it's Hard to be the Disciplinarian"

A final factor making the application of discipline difficult is the dynamic of single parenthood. I could write a whole book for the single parent. I love single parents. My heart goes out to them and I pray for the single parents I work with all the time. I was a single parent for a time while raising my daughters and my respect multiplied a thousand times as I struggled to work full time and be at events, get my daughters to the doctor, arrange sick days and sleepovers, and stay on top of lunches, homework, and field trips. Much like Forrest Gump discovered about shrimping ("Shrimpin' is tough!") I found out "Single parenting is tough!" Only the bravest of the brave tread these paths; only the strongest in heart, mind, and will traverse this terrain and come out the other side. I cannot tell you the tears, pain, and emotional devastation I have helped to unload from moms, dads, and grandparents as they try to be "everything" for their child or adolescent. Society has not been kind to single parents, nor has the field of psychology and counseling. It was believed for many years single parents could not meet their children's needs adequately; and children who grew up in single parent homes were handicapped in some way. Thankfully, this ridiculous notion has been blown out of the water, but the residue still exists in many arenas and communities who hold to this archaic thinking. I still talk to single parents who with tears in their eyes say to me, "Well, I know it will hurt him because…I'm a woman and he is a boy…She's a girl and I'm a man…" and on and on. I work hard to show them with love and firm boundaries that their child will have all he or she needs. Yes, even a child diagnosed with AS/HFA! In fact, I give them homework to find all the successful people in our world who grew up without a mother, father, or neither.

Applying discipline is usually a complicated issue for single parents, because the single parent wears so many "hats." Many single moms, dads, and grandparents struggle to find a balance between being the friend, teacher, playmate, meal maker, maid, taxi driver and whatever else the child needs. Children are often shocked and hurt when a parent who has been a "buddy" suddenly sends them to bed early because they did not do their homework. Single parents are often overworked and in a constant state of emotional stress as a result of the extra physical, emotional, mental, and financial demands of raising children alone. I find the last thing on their minds is finding appropriate consequences for negative behavior, and usually by the time they come to me, there are a great deal of bad habits have already formed. For single parents of children and adolescents diagnosed with AS/HFA, there is an even greater burden. I have written this section to help the single parent of children and adolescents diagnosed with AS/HFA and to give them hope and encouragement. Again, my purpose here is to keep things simple and clear, and there are some principles that can help.

First, the parent needs a "playbook." Similar to the previous section, the parent needs to have a system of rewards and consequences in place prior to dealing with negative behavior that is clear, understood by the child or adolescent, and one the parent is not afraid to implement. When a parent waits until something happens to try and find an appropriate consequence, it usually does not go well. We must remember the purpose of applying consequences is to teach our child something, not because we are angry or embarrassed or want "revenge" for how frustrated we can become in trying to deal with poor behavior choices. The appendix section has a list of resources to help with discipline, but I will summarize a few helpful techniques to keep in mind.

1. Do not attempt to provide consequences when you are emotionally aroused. Anger and frustration only send confusing messages, especially for children and adolescents diagnosed with AS/HFA. Wait until you are calm. You can say to your child, "Your behavior was inappropriate and I am going to give you a consequence, but I do not know what that will be right now. I will let you know in a little while."

2. Do not use consequences or rewards as threats. Be clear and follow through.

3. Do not lecture once the consequence is given. Let the young person feel the weight of learning something through the consequence and save your words

and energy. If you feel the need to "review" what happened, do so after the consequence has been given and served.

4.   If you take away a privilege, always provide a time frame (the shorter the better) and always give the opportunity to earn it back and provide clear and simple steps for earning back the privilege. Children and adolescents will work harder to make good choices to earn something back than working for something that may be "gone forever." By providing a time frame the child or adolescent can see a "goal" and will work to change behavior (and learn something) rather than learning to live without whatever privilege was taken away.

5.   Focus on rewarding positive behaviors instead of focusing on giving consequences for negative behaviors. Keeping a positive mindset takes much less energy and children and adolescents tend to respond better to positive reinforcement than negative.

6.   Remember the purpose of providing consequences is to teach. Before giving a consequence, ask yourself "What is my child or adolescent going to learn from this?" and "What am I trying to teach him or her?" This helps keep you on course and also helps you to eliminate negative emotions that may impair your ability to find a good consequence. For example, if you are very angry at your child, your consequence is likely to be more severe and teach less than if you are clear headed and calm.

7.   Do not negotiate once the consequence is given. Be firm and be clear: "I will talk with you later after you have completed your extra chore. Bye." Send the message that the child earned the extra chore through poor choices and the time for explaining is over, and if he completes the chore, then he can talk about it at that time. It is natural for young people to want to get out of consequences (they are just like us!) and their desire to talk is usually a last-minute effort to get out of work. Be firm, and walk away.

8.   Adopt an attitude that applying consequences helps build responsibility for your child or adolescent. You are not a "meanie" for holding them responsible when she does not make positive choices. Even though AS/HFA presents a great deal of challenges for young people, it should be the goal of any parent of one of these amazing young people to help them become as independent as possible and to help them understand the principle that good choices brings good rewards.

9. Remember you, the parent, have "Veto" power at all times. There may be extenuating circumstances that change the level of the consequence or one may not be needed at all. You know your child better than anyone and you have the right to alter the consequences or not give one based on what you think and feel at the time.

10. Do not invite the input of siblings in this process. Make this about you the parent being in control and sending the message that you are the authority figure. Keep this boundary firm and clear to all the young people in the family system.

A second helpful principle is the single parent must have firm and clear boundaries. Much has been written about "boundaries" and it is still a buzzword in pop-psychology. Many people view this as telling people "off" when they get angry, but the concept of boundaries is much different. What I mean by firm and clear boundaries for the single parent of a child or adolescent diagnosed with AS/HFA is being able to send the message to your child or adolescent that while you wear many hats (playmate, provider, housekeeper, grocery getter, etc.) your main role is to teach and guide the child or adolescent and prepare him or her for life's journey. Having boundaries does not mean that you are cold and aloof. In fact, having solid boundaries means you are free to engage and connect with your child or adolescent even more. You can definitely play with your child and still have boundaries. You can definitely be silly on a Friday night and put on your pajamas and dance around the living room and still have boundaries. The point is that the child or adolescent diagnosed with AS/HFA needs to know you are his protector, teacher, and guide (and one that is willing to be fun and play along the way) and sometimes your role will be to push him towards growth and that you are willing to do so when the situation calls for it.

A third and final principle is that the single parent of a child or adolescent diagnosed with AS/HFA needs to "Get a Life!" I am not saying this in a judgmental or mean way, but in an empowering way. I tell all the single parents I work with to "Get a Life," which means to have your own set of hobbies, interests, and social network outside of your child. Too many single parents create a world only involving their child. Thus, many children of single parents think the parent's sole purpose is to serve them and the parent is turned into an object instead of a real person. Over time, the parent's social contacts are their child's friend's parents; the only places the parent goes are related to their child (park, school, swim class, etc.); the only time these parents have fun is when their child is having fun. I hear stories of parents who are longing to go hiking, fishing, do scrap-booking, write a novel (just to name a few) and when I ask them why they have not done these things, they respond with a downtrodden look, "I don't have time because my child takes up so much of my time." "Excuses!" I say. I am not trying to embarrass them, nor do I want to minimize their commitment to give all their time to their child. I am simply trying to get them to expand their view of life from a narrow, tunnel vision mindset to a larger, and more free and open viewpoint. I have written in an earlier section how parents of special needs children tend to see the child as fragile and the parents are so used to being ready at a minute's notice to attend to all the needs of their child that the parent gives up all their interests and social relationships to focus on the needs of their child. Parents of children and adolescents diagnosed with AS/HFA can easily fall into this way of thinking, and while parenting in general calls for sacrifice, parents should still retain an identity separate from their child. If not, the child may become overly dependent on the parent or the parent may become overly depended on the child and use the child as the parent's source of emotional support. This dynamic can easily develop for single parents and especially for the single parent raising a child diagnosed with AS/HFA. This "enmeshment" can stunt the child's growth and keep him or her from developing emotionally and socially, and can cause other problems as the child nears adulthood.

So what does "Getting a Life" look like you may ask? It means allowing yourself the freedom to get a sitter for your child and to have a few hours for yourself. It means letting your child see you going off with "your friends" to have fun, whatever that fun may be. It means sending the message to your child or adolescent and you have a whole life outside of the child or adolescent's world, and while you love your child or adolescent very much, your world does not revolve around him or her. It means you get to do something you love that "recharges your batteries" and makes you an even better parent when you reunite with your child. It also means that on a regular basis, your child or adolescent must accept the fact he will be left in the care of others so you can go pursue an interest of yours. This is important because it helps to solidify your identity as more than your child or adolescent's servant and sole companion, and also serves to model for your child or adolescent diagnosed with AS/HFA connection with other people and organizations. Another positive of single parents showing their child or adolescent they have outside interests is it can help to move the young person towards independence and self-confidence.

The Art of Restoring and Sustaining the Relationship through the Discipline Process

Perhaps the greatest reason parents do not like dealing with disciplining their child's poor choices is the negative feelings that are directed toward the parent by the child or adolescent once a consequence has been given. Children carry an immense fear of being abandoned by their parents; but I find many parents carry an immense fear of being abandoned by their children. Even the strongest of parents tend to crumble at the sound of a slammed door and those dreaded words: "I hate you!!!" I constantly remind parents in my office that a child's or adolescent's anger comes from personal embarrassment and frustration about the situation; it is not about the parent. In fact, children and adolescents like knowing boundaries are present, even though they may buck against the "fence" these consequence provides. I doubt anyone likes getting a speeding ticket; however, there is a sense of relief knowing a law enforcement system is in place, especially when one needs the assistance of the law. This is the same feeling young people experience when they receive a consequence. On the one hand it is somewhat painful and annoying; on the other, it is a reminder that they are loved and protected. When a consequence is given, they are usually angry and frustrated at the circumstance and situation; these negative feelings are directed towards the parent and usually interpreted by the parent in a negative manner. This is where things usually turn out badly. The parent either "explodes" at the child or adolescent's negative reactions, creating even more negative emotions and emotional wounds (and possibly, physical) by yelling back at the young person and escalating the situation. The young person actually buys time with this scenario because the parent "took the bait" and is now in a yelling match that serves to take the focus off of the young person's poor choices and the consequence. Additionally, the parent now appears foolish and out of control, which places the young person at the helm of the situation. The other scenario is when the parent crumbles at the sight of the young person's emotional reaction and withdraws the consequence and either engages in "negotiation" with the child, lessens the consequence, or removes it all together. Once again, this places the child or adolescent in control and gives him what he wants and teaches the child he can "wiggle" out of consequences through emotional and behavioral reactions, reinforcing the fact that the parent does not follow through with what the parents say they are going to do.

For children and adolescents diagnosed with AS/HFA, either of the above scenarios is disastrous. These young people have difficulty interpreting emotions and facial expressions of others and when a parent reacts, the only message many of these people get is, "My parent hates me." When parents do not follow through with consequences, the young person diagnosed with AS/HFA receives a mixed message: Sometimes behaviors are excused; sometimes they are not. Young people diagnosed with AS/HFA have difficulty seeing things from a different perspective (mind-blindness) and can often be confusing when the parent does not follow through. However, when a parent is consistent with a system of rewards and consequences, the young person diagnosed with AS/HFA usually responds well, as these young people tend to like rules and operational systems. What follows in this section is a clear and simple guideline to help you, the parent, sustain relationship and connection with your child or adolescent diagnosed with AS/HFA while applying consequences and restoring the relationship following the delivery of consequences.

Keeping the Bridge Strong: Sustaining the Relationship through the Discipline Process

The theme of this book is about building connection with your child or adolescent diagnosed with AS/HFA. My hope in writing this section is to show parents that building connection is not just something that is done in the easy times when things are smooth, but also during times of struggle and trials. Raising a child diagnosed with AS/HFA certainly is not an easy task; and many parents I talk with tell me they are tired and discouraged. Many live in fear that their young person will never be independent and will not find a place to fit in society. As I have written earlier in this chapter, applying consequences to help shape the young person's behavior and build independence can bring struggles and trials in the form of emotional outbursts and negative behaviors. However, a calm and stable parent base serves to stabilize the environment of the young person, which in turn will provide a sense of safety and comfort for the child or adolescent that will be experienced as a result of the parent's wisdom and consistency. There are a few simple steps to follow that will help you keep the bridge strong.

Be Non-Reactive!

I have written repeatedly about this one constant theme of being non-reactive, and it applies here. I cannot emphasize this one concept enough, especially when it comes to parents raising children and adolescents diagnosed with AS/HFA.

The power of this concept is when the parent commits to not react to the child or adolescent's behavior or emotions, the foundation of the relationship bridge holds firm. There is emotional wounding or confusion that often results from yelling, screaming, slamming things, and the worst of all, physical harm. However, as a parent myself, and one who works with young people all day, I know this is much easier said than done. One thing I have learned for myself and I seek to teach other parents is to "reframe" the young person's behavior or emotional outburst. Instead of interpreting it as an attack on me and making it a personal matter, I must change my thinking and see the child's reactivity as a fear-based, emotionally immature response that is complicated by the challenges of AS/HFA. Through reframing, my "fight-or-flight" response is not triggered and I am able to stay present in the moment. This is a very powerful and effective way to be "non-reactive" and is another reason why I spend so much time talking about the brain, "fight-or-flight," and how a parent's reactivity is like throwing gasoline on a fire.

The second part of being "non-reactive" involves controlling the physical response of the body through relaxation of the core muscles. This is the technique I wrote about in Chapter Three. When a parent combines this with the cognitive reframing mentioned above, a powerful presence is created and the "fight-or-flight" response is overridden. The parent stays in "thinking" mode and appears much like "Spock" in the old Star Trek series, not rocked by emotions or chaos. The young person sees a parent who is firm, but also loving, a parent who is wise and in control, who speaks calmly and gently, and who reinforces the idea that rules must be followed and order maintained. The young person sees a parent who is safe, predictable, and approachable. The young person also sees a parent who leads by example, which is a powerful thing for our young people who are developing and moving towards adulthood. I challenge each parent raising a child or adolescent diagnosed with AS/HFA to commit to being non-reactive at all times, no matter what the circumstances and no matter how intense the behavioral or emotional outburst of the child or adolescent.

Use Words of Love and Encouragement in the Discipline Process

In addition to being non-reactive, a parent must be able to communicate effectively through the discipline process. This is not easy because of the emotional eruption of the young person that sometimes occurs following the delivery of a consequence.

Through reframing the child or adolescent's reaction and by physically releasing tension in the core muscles, the parent can override the natural impulse to react towards or get away from the child and stay in the moment with the child by adopting a non-reactive presence. The second piece of sustaining connection through the discipline process is to use words of love and encouragement. Our voices are powerful and the tones of our voices communicate a great deal and also serve to calm a tense situation. Early in my career in the mental health field I worked at an inpatient hospital with patients suffering from intense emotional and psychological trauma. The first thing I was taught was the volume and tone of my voice and the words I choose could de-escalate a potentially violent situation and help a patient who was delusional either pull out of the delusional state, or at least keep the person from hurting himself or someone else. I learned a calm and firm tone coupled with words that were directive, reassuring, and kind could prevent a physical intervention ninety percent of the time. This training proved invaluable as I began working full time with young people and families, and it formed a deep commitment within me to assure my own children I would never raise my voice with them or use words that hurt, are mean spirited, or wound. I am committed to never tell a parent something I have not put into practice in my own life, and I strive each day to live what I teach. Many parents, especially those who have grown up in chaotic households, use yelling and threats of physical force because it is what their brain interprets as the normal response when children or adolescents are "acting up." I never judge these parents harshly, but I show them there is another way and I am patient in my persistence in encouraging them to change their words and tones to those of firmness, gentleness, love, and encouragement. No young person comes into the world fully equipped to make all the right choices, manage emotions, and zoom through the developmental stages in a "perfect" manner. So why do parents seem shocked when a young person lies? Why do parents "freak out" when a homework assignment is not turned in? When a young person attempts to sneak out at night? We learn by making mistakes and we rely on our parents to show us the boundaries when we cannot find them. And young people learn best when the teacher (parent) is calm, firm, and sending a message of love and safety.

I have found children and adolescents diagnosed with AS/HFA tend to be more curious about things than most young people. These amazing young people have a great deal of energy and pursue their interests with a "white-hot" intensity which to me is completely amazing. However, in their curiosity coupled with the zeal for knowledge, things are likely to get broken, torn apart in a chaotic manner, and the task of putting tools back where they were found and cleaning up messes is not a top priority. I have met young people diagnosed with AS/HFA who took apart the family computer just to see the "guts" because they were intrigued by the inside components. Neither of the young people in this situation set out to "ruin the parent's day" but it sure felt like it for the poor parents who found the dismantled components of a very expensive and necessary device all over the living room. How would you handle this? Would you be able to reframe it, stay calm, and use words of firmness and love in order to teach or would you "freak out?" Certainly, a scenario such as this would likely test even the most seasoned professional not to mention a parent. Now imagine in fifteen years the very same young person invents a new technological component that transforms the computer industry and results in making the person a billionaire overnight. This is the vision parents need in situation like this. Yes, this scenario would test us all; however, despite how frustrating this would be, it is an opportunity to teach, connect, and channel the curiosity of the young person towards a positive outlet.

You may be asking, what do words of love and encouragement sound like during the discipline process? Here are a few examples:

"You have made a wrong choice and I'm sorry that you have done that. You are going to receive a consequence to help you remember how to make a good choice. I care about you and want you to learn how to make good choices."

"I can see that you are upset, but I want to remind you that I love you and that you are safe. Once you calm down, I'll be here to help you once your voice sounds like mine."

"I love you enough to help you make good choices. You might be angry with me but that is o.k. I will not leave you and I know that you know how to make good choices. Once you complete your extra chores we can have some fun together. Let me know when you are done."

"I am so proud of you for making good choices. I knew that you could do it, please come tell me when you feel overwhelmed and we can talk about it."

These examples show how words of love and encouragement coupled with a calm tone provide reassurance to the child while the parent models for the child how to put feelings into words and to also control emotional and behavioral reactions.

Body Language: When Words and Behaviors Match

While verbal responses help to soothe a tense situation, body language also plays a role. Our bodies communicate a great deal. I can tell someone I love them very much but if my arms are folded and brow is furrowed, the person is likely to doubt the sincerity of my statement. For connection to be sustained through the discipline process, the parent's body language must also communicate calmness, caring, and a non-threatening presence. Some of the parents I work with tell me they communicate what I have presented here, but they have done so through clenched teeth. "But I said what you told me to say!" they remark, and I tell them the angry, taut face and clenched teeth probably sent a double message. I tell them it probably appeared to the child as "I'm telling you this, but I don't really mean it." I have found children and adolescents diagnosed with AS/HFA pay attention to body language and are sensitive to the physical manner that adults portray. In my experience, many of these young people are expert "people watchers," and one of the first things I do when I meet one in my office is to be careful of my body language. I never try to tower over them (I'm six feet one inch) or sit too close; I often sit on the floor so that they are taller than I am. I often have some blocks nearby or a ball that I roll around on the floor so they see my hands are safe and that I like to use my hands to build things or play. I am cautious not to stare or make direct eye contact for too long; I smile a lot and look out the window while I am talking. Through my physical presence, I am sending a message to the child or adolescent that I am safe and non-threatening; I want them to see me as someone who can be trusted.

Body language is important in the restorative process following the delivery of consequences. While many young people diagnosed with AS/HFA do not like to be touched or hugged, though, many do and I have found parents have been able to utilize this as part of the discipline process by communicating to the child that the child is loved and that this love was not lost even though the young person made a wrong choice. This concept of unconditional love to me is one of the most important foundations of building a child's sense of self-worth and confidence; the thought of "No matter what I do I cannot lose my parent's love" creates a deep force deep within the child. From this foundation comes the ability to dream, dare mighty things, and seek to do one's very best in all situations. This foundational concept creates the opportunity for emotional, mental, and social growth and the ability to eliminate fear. For young people who do not like to be touched, the parent can still physically be around the young person and portray an open, non-threatening stance. Children and adolescents diagnosed with AS/HFA can be confused by body language and often interpret body language differently than neurotypical individuals. Regardless, parents must be sure that their facial expression and body stance communicates gentleness, firmness, and relationship restoration once the delivery of consequences is complete. I will now use a few case examples to further explain how restoring and sustaining the connection works in the discipline process.

Eager Beaver

Like many young people diagnosed with AS/HFA, James, a twelve year old boy, loved mechanical things and liked to figure out how things work. His father, Max, a "jack of all trades" had many tools and was good at fixing things. He was a "tinkerer" and noticed James' similar interests in mechanical components and discovering how things work. One day, while James' parents were entertaining company, James went out into the garage and began to take apart his father's very expensive riding lawn mower. After an hour of not knowing where James was, his father went out into the garage and found engine parts strewn over parts of the garage and driveway. Walking a bit further, he found James, grinning, with grease and oil on his hands, face, and shirt and very proudly held up a piece of the engine. "I finally figured it out, Dad! There is a belt that connects the engine to the mower blades and that is what makes it spin!" Max immediately walked away, and gave a feeble reply, "Okay, buddy. I'll be right back." "Where are you going?" James asked in a confused tone. Max did not answer. He was feeling faint, and blood was pounding in his head. Max took some deep breaths and walked into the back yard. Finally, his vision cleared and the blood stopped pounding. That mower was his pride and joy; he would have to put it back together, if he could put it back together. He wanted to yell. James had done this before with the coffee pot, the blender, most anything that had a motor in it, and usually the item was nearly ruined mainly because James did not use the right tools to take it apart. He was simply so eager to see the "guts" of the item that he tore into it with reckless abandon. In recent years, Max had begun teaching James about tools and had involved James in some of his work. Max had calmed down, but was still feeling anger and frustration, and then suddenly, a thought hit him. He was James at about twelve; he was curious, but his father was not very kind. He rarely let Max use tools, which led to Max sneaking them and then his father would find out and take the belt to him, which only fueled Max's desire to not get caught. Suddenly, Max felt a softening inside himself. James did not do this to hurt Max or to destroy the mower; he was curious and was investigating. In fact, Max remembered James saying he believed he could take apart the mower and put it back together. Focusing on the positive, Max noted James had not been hurt, the mower was fixable, and James had skills that would one day possibly form into a career.

Suddenly, Max felt a smile creeping towards the corners of his mouth. He had been looking for a new way to connect with James and now he found it. Going back around the house he found James still sitting in the driveway, admiring his work. He plopped down next to him and firmly told James he needed to talk with him. He made sure James was listening. He calmly told James the behavior he chose was wrong and Max wondered if James could tell him why it was wrong. Slowly, James told his father he had used the tools without permission and he was supposed to ask before taking something apart. Max praised James for being able to put his thoughts into words, and then he asked James, "What do we have to do now?" James told his father the mower needed to be put back together and eagerly told his father he could do it. Max told him, "Well, we do need to put it together, but those who want to use my tools must ask permission first. So we are going to leave all this here for now. I want you to go inside and get cleaned up and get on your computer and see if you can find this type of mower and an owner's manual with the listing of parts. Most companies post owner's manuals online because they don't want to waste the paper anymore. Once you pull that up, come find me and after our guests have gone we'll get busy out here. I'm going to show you how to properly rebuild something. Do you understand?" Max hugged James after saying this and James affirmed to Max that he understood and went inside. Max followed and with one last look at the mess in the garage, shut the door and took a few deep breaths before rejoining his wife and their guests in the living room.

Discussion of Eager Beaver

Notice Max felt frustration and anger and also the urge to react, but he walked away for a short time. Sometimes, this is the best initial option. While nothing is dealt with or solved, the parent is able to get himself under control first, and then the parent is more ready to deal with the situation. Max was very wise here because this moment turned out to be one of those "golden" moments in which father and son built a deeper connection and James' interest in mechanics and tools blossomed because he felt he had the freedom to pursue it, based on Max's controlled reaction. Had Max exploded, James more than likely would not have made the connection to the *why* Dad was mad, but instead his thinking would have likely been "Dad is mad, he must hate me". Neurotypical individuals, especially parents, feel justified in "blowing up" because they assume the young person is going to know the why of the situation through seeing the parent's angry reaction. Most parents react because they believe the reaction is what will communicate *"You have done something wrong and don't ever do it again!"* and the incident will be over. Certainly for children and adolescents diagnosed with AS/HFA this is counterproductive because of mind-blindness and alexithymia, but it is also counterproductive for neurotypical children and adolescents as well. When a parent yells and reacts in a negative emotional manner, the child's defenses go up and the ability of the child to learn becomes disrupted.

Notice also Max's words and behavior matched perfectly. It is not enough for parents simply speak in a calm voice, but their behavior match what the words being spoken. Max was calm, and his words were communicating "It's okay; we can fix this," but he also sat on the ground with James and his body language matched his words. His face was calm and relaxed; his voice flowed smoothly and evenly. By sitting James on the ground, Max joined James where he was. Max did not stand over him, did not pace frantically back and forth, or use an intimidating posture. Again, his body language matched the words and tone, and the relationship between Max and James was not only sustained and restored, but it was also strengthened. Note also that following the conversation, Max gave James a hug, which also reinforced the fact the relationship was restored. Your young person may not like hugs and if he does not, I do not recommend using a time such as this initiate one. However, you know your child best and I recommend you consider some form of physical gesture he is comfortable with to make a connection. After this event, Max and James "tinkered" together on a regular basis each week. Max found old electrical appliances and small engines for himself and James to dismantle, and he showed James how to take things apart in an orderly manner, and also how to drain various oils and fluids from different components.

Frustrated Son, Frustrated Mom

Allen was a ten year old boy diagnosed with AS/HFA who lived with his mother Joyce and their dog Samson. Allen's father had abandoned the family when Allen was a baby, Joyce had dated a few times but found taking care of Allen was all she wanted and needed at this stage of her life. Allen loved the rigidness of routine and hated to deviate from anything other than "the plan." He would ask his mother each day for reassurance, making sure the day would go according to "the plan." When there was a deviation from "the plan" because of unforeseen circumstances, Allen would become hysterical and cry and flail about; once Allen hit his mother in his blind rage. This tantrum routine had become so severe Joyce had decided to home-school Allen because these "fits" had become more common as the social and emotional pressure at school increased with each new grade level. Working from home, she was able to be with him most of the time, and because she loved Allen so much, she worked hard to follow his chosen routine to the letter. However, her work situation changed and the company she worked for called on her to be in the field more, which completely threw Allen off balance emotionally and behaviorally. His outbursts had become so severe she had to cancel her field work and was in danger of losing her job. When she explained this to Allen he yelled, "Your job is to be with me!!!" The more she tried to explain the more frustrated he became and then Joyce became an emotional mess. Both mother and son were very hurt and frustrated.

Because of Allen's outbursts and difficulty in social situations, she found a clinical counselor to work with Allen to help him with these issues. The counselor told her Allen's behavior was typical for a young person diagnosed with AS/HFA; however, the counselor was concerned and unless something changed, Allen may get "stuck" in his routines and his fear was Allen would never be able to adjust to a circumstance out of his control, which would have devastating effects as he neared adulthood. The counselor suggested making small changes, giving Joyce the vision to gradually shape Allen's thinking and behavior much like one would do with a young tree. Too much change would break Allen, but small amounts here and there could gradually help him learn to adjust and also would align nicely with the mental and emotional maturity that was in the process of developing. The counselor worked with Allen individually and gradually formed a strong, trusting relationship with him that enabled the counselor to help Allen with his fears and worries. Like many children diagnosed with AS/HFA, Allen exhibited obsessive, compulsive behaviors to help soothe his fears and worries, and the counselor began teaching Allen some techniques to self-soothe without the need for the rigid schedule. The counselor developed strategies and techniques to help Joyce teach Allen in the home environment to gradually learn to accept changes out of his control. Some of these included creating a weekly schedule with minor changes built in so Allen knew what changes were going to be implemented and was aware of them ahead of time. Another technique was offering Allen choices when a situation arose, helping him feel in control. For example, when he could not have his favorite pasta for lunch, Allen was able to choose between chicken noodle soup and tuna fish sandwich. These were foods he liked but were not his first choice for lunch, but once he was put in charge of making the choice he felt somewhat in control. This situation is just one example how a gradual shift in Allen's environment helped to reinforce what he was being taught in his individual counseling sessions.

To no one's surprise, there were some struggles for Allen and his mother during this process. Allen fought every step of the way initially; however, the one main difference was Joyce had ceased becoming emotional with Allen; instead, she had learned to be non-reactive and in the beginning Allen did not like this. Again, this is not because he was "bad" or "oppositional defiant;" it was because he worked hard to control his environment because it helped him feel safe. Through being non-reactive, Joyce felt more in control when Allen became emotional and had the energy to deliver consequences when he made poor choices. Gradually, she broke Allen's dependent hold on her and gradually shifted him to become more self-reliant and independent. One day, Joyce had to go into the field and had arranged for Allen to have a teacher come and conduct his math and history lesson while she was gone. Allen began to tantrum, screaming and thrashing his body around on the floor. Joyce remained calm and immediately left the room to continue getting ready. Allen followed and again began the tantrum behavior all over again on her bedroom floor. "I can't be around you when you are choosing this behavior," Joyce stated in a matter of fact tone. "Please go to your room to calm down and then you can tell me what is bothering you." Allen's wailing increased and he continued to thrash. "I'm going to the living room now and when you are calm you may come with me," Joyce stated as she stepped over him to leave the room. She went to the living room and calmly began putting her things together to go to work. Allen stopped wailing and flailing and watched her, tears running down his face and his chest heaving with sobs. Three months prior to this, Allen probably would have continued wailing and might have grabbed Joyce to keep her from leaving the room. However, he has gradually stopped this type of behavior as Joyce was more firm and consistent. "Would you like to sit with me for a few minutes?" Joyce asked. Allen nodded and cuddled next to her. Joyce wrapped her arms around him. "I know you don't like me to go, and I don't like to either, but I need to work a little today. Miss Amy will be here in a few minutes and there is something I want to tell you, ok?" "I don't want Miss Amy to come: I want you," Allen whined. "Well, tonight I am going to be home by five o'clock and we are going to go on our bike ride after dinner, (Allen loved bike riding with Mom) how does that sound?" Allen's eyes perked up. "Good," he said. "So, if you can get your work done this afternoon, then we can go on our bike ride tonight, ok?" "Yeah, that will be fun," Allen responded. "Ok good," said Joyce, "Now we need to clean up a little before Miss Amy comes. Come along and I'll help you in the bathroom." Allen took his mother's hand and walked with her to the bathroom.

Discussion of Frustrated Son, Frustrated Mom

Notice the progression of Joyce gradually pulling away from Allen in small increments. This needs to be done slowly; too much too soon and it can be traumatic for the child or adolescent diagnosed with AS/HFA. Joyce committed to being firm and consistent, yet she maintained communication of love and her body language matched her words perfectly. She knew Allen inside and out and used her knowledge of how he "ticked" to both connect with him through the process, but also to deliver consequences and set boundaries. Over time, she was able to gradually change the dynamics of their relationship but did not do so in an angry or passive aggressive manner. Small changes, implemented gradually, coupled with connection and relationship served not only to preserve the relationship between Joyce and Allen, but also moved him up the developmental ladder. Joyce noticed Allen was able to adjust to changes in many different situations, and he no longer panicked when she was not immediately available. This separation laid the foundation for Allen to join some social groups in the community like a chess club and Boy Scouts, and he became more independent and confident in himself.

The Family Meeting

One final tool I recommend for all parents who want to build connection with their children is to implement the "Family Meeting." I observed the power of this when I was employed at a local Children's Home where I served in a cottage with eight different children from eight different backgrounds. The family meeting is a time where all the members of the family come together and each person is given a chance to voice a question, comment, or concern. The member might share a funny story about his day; another member might share something that made her feel sad; or a member might share an issue that is bothering him regarding their sibling sitting next to him. No one else can speak while the selected family member is speaking, unless the content of what they are saying becomes inappropriate. The parents may share the plan for the evening or the upcoming weekend, or can share a funny story as well. The family meeting serves two very important purposes: 1) The parents are reaffirmed their place as leaders and teachers; and 2) The young people are provided a place where they can speak and be heard.

I was astounded by how the family meeting connected our cottage members, and also helped to establish the staff as professional, competent, yet caring and supportive. Conflict between cottage mates was often resolved during the family meeting and instead of a staff member playing "referee" during a squabble between two unhappy housemates, the staff member would remark "Let's talk about that during family meeting." I have seen this work well with families by helping to build connection between siblings and to make the young people feel like they have a voice. I have seen parents who previously felt out of control be able to re-establish themselves as the authority figures, not in a tyrannical manner, but with firmness, gentleness, and love. The family meeting is also a great time to discuss changes in the family system such as a new routine or homework schedule, chore assignments, or new consequences for poor behavior choices and new rewards for positive behavior choices. I remind parents this is a great way to build connection, model effective communication, and teach conflict resolution. While it is impossible for most families to conduct a family meeting each day, I suggest at least three times per week for this tool to be effective. Trust me, you will be amazed at how effective this tool can be!

Epilogue

Writing this book is a great honor for me, and I hope you find the information contained herein to be useful. I strive each day to do my very best in working with children and adolescents diagnosed with AS/HFA and their families, and building connection is perhaps the greatest "tool" in my work. Relationships sustain us; our connections with those around us are what give our lives meaning, as it is nearly impossible to get through life completely alone. When we dare to scrape away our material possessions and take an honest look at what is most important in our lives, we always come back to relationships. Ask someone who has lived through a devastating tornado in the Midwest; someone who has live through a hurricane in the south; and someone who has lost a loved one to cancer or some other dreadful disease or accident. Nothing replaces relationship. "Stuff" is nice, but "stuff" cannot hug you or carry on a conversation. "Stuff" cannot replace the sincerity or support of a real human being.

I challenge you today, right here and now to begin working on building relationship and connection with your child or adolescent diagnosed with AS/HFA. Do not believe the myth that these young people do not want or need relationship; or the myth that these young people are robots with no feelings. No, far from it, not these young people. In fact, the young people I come in contact with continue to amaze me as they communicate to me their deep desire for relationship and connection; they just get a little lost on the way to the goal. Discouraging at times? Yes. Overwhelming? Absolutely. But take a deep breath, refocus, and get back in that ring. Live in the "miracle of now" and do not let another moment go by. Your child, your adolescent is waiting, and he or she needs you so very much. Have fun on your journey and do not forget you are never, ever alone!

Kevin B. Hull
March 29, 2012

Johnny's Letter

Dear Mum and Dad,

I actually deeply, authentically, and completely LOVE you Mum and Dad. Really. Knock, knock? Who's there? ME! There really IS someone home here Mum and Dad.

And I'll let you into my world – slowly – gently – quietly... but you just **gotta remember** that bit about *"when in Rome"*...

Occasionally I see that water trickle from your eyes, that sigh-breath thing you do, the slumped head-in-hands bit – that's you suspecting that because of my rather scarce emotional displays you're having doubts about my love. Don't doubt. You see,

I don't do that sort of emotional display easily. Hugs often hurt. Kisses – yuck. Love is a decision, not mushy stuff for me... and I've long decided for YOU. Both of you. Guess what? You're my world too.

Still, sometimes I detect that *you know I love you*, but even then don't expect me to say it out loud, that would be a 'horribly inefficient duplication' of feelings... and a painful intense emotional interrupt to my functioning. An interruption to my need to manage internal temperatures, my anxieties, the coursing of powerful and even overwhelming feelings. Saying it out loud is a disabling brain activity. IQ-lowering stuff.

Yet, who do I talk to, stand with, go to, trust, show things to, think aloud to, sit with, cry in front of? No more misinterpretations, please: I am constantly saying "I love you, I love you, **I love YOU**" – that's all!

I know I seldom seem to listen *in the moment*. I know, but I do listen very very carefully, *even then*. That's why I know so much. (Sometimes too much). Draw me a picture - I will photograph it and etch it deeply in white brain cells. Make me a book - I will chant it inside till known off-by-heart. I drink deeply from the well of who you are. I am after all a Repository of Information and Abider of Rules. Especially yours... and I really hear you in a way that, perhaps, no other can.

Don't be fooled by the merchants of glibness, money-makers, snake-oil merchants... for some are nothing short of purveyors of death... you see, I am **NOT** my behaviour. Never have been. That's just the stained and ripped book cover *(someone else did it - not me)*. You see I have this long story inside me and it sort of encompasses my feelings and thoughts. All that has ever happened to me, all of the indescribable parts of me no one can see merely by "observing my behaviour", how and why I soar and plummet wildly, my thirst for justice and a sense of well-being, the euphoria I feel observing tiny rain drops on velour furred roses - and equally - spotting three ghastly matching weeds stood at attention in a neat row...everything, yes, everything. I do not want "how it all comes out" to define our relationship. I am much much more than that. You AND me both, eh!

I am not an alien, but you can help me to avoid being *alienated*. First by acknowledging you are weird to me too. Weird as. Except maybe Dad sometimes? Or maybe it's Mum whose strange at times? My genetic composition didn't come from outta nowhere y'know. You are even different from others of your own kind! Can we celebrate every single one of those differences together? Let's get out the crystal glasses and decanter kept in the special cupboard (the one I used to be fascinated with)... and drink merrily to that today!

While we're on that point about you being extra weird Dad, Mum, can one of you or both consider getting a diagnosis and publishing it in the newspaper for all to see? Esteem isn't built on back-patting and soothing affirmations alone. Sometimes we just gotta nail our colours to a very public mast. Sometimes we all gotta.

And if you don't get a diagnosis Dad or Mum, OK, but please leave me to "know" Autism. Do not claim to "know" it like I know it. Your job is to help me. To feel with me and all that stuff, but not to replace me - heh, not even on the local branch of my own autism organization!

You sometimes seriously underestimate the challenges I face most minutes of the day. Challenges created by my associated comorbids. Sometimes you are blinded by my abilities and forget my conditions' inherent complexities and all the apparent contradictions and paradoxes in Autism and Asperger's. You sometimes overlook my skill at surmounting these 'wicked' challenges, because of my resilience, my strategising and my ability to focus. Keep the balance guys. Please don't trip.

I learnt to spell words to show I am not retarded. Big words like "incontestable proof" and "paradoxical contradiction" and little words like "shove it" too. I know so much more than is seen in 'regular' communication. Communication I find so difficult to use. Communication that never seems enough to portray the 'meanings' I want to express - the exactnesses, the sensory connections, the whole of what I feel so outrageously inside.

Sometimes I need a rest from Asperger's Syndrome and Autism. Know what I mean? When I turn 18 and drink a little too much, I'm also gonna wanna be mainly legless for a while. OK? I want the dignity that comes from making similar mistakes to others. So, ah, let go appropriately. But don't let me stay in denial or always hide behind the non-appearance of my condition to satisfy some peer manipulation or any fears - I have some nailing up of colours to do also... eventually.

If you are going to help me do something, please make damned sure that your intention is that I'm gonna do it all my self later on. I embrace autonomy and independence... about as much as you let me... once my inertia is overcome. Sink or swim as an adult... it's up to you. Just like it is for every other child in the world too I guess.

Do not pay too much attention to any 'Triad of Impairments' – they are as valuable as zookeeper observations about monkeys at a tea party, well, to me anyway. Asperger's is much more about perspectives, preferences, porous timekeeping, profound focus, party foods, and being practically beaten up everyday by bullies. Really.

Asperger's is about processing information in different parts of the brain than 'typical' people and 'feeling' every sensory sensation. It's about 'seeing' the beauty found in all the details my brain doesn't get to filter out. The experts say I'm 'in my own world' but without all the brain filters removing so called 'unnecessary information', I'm actually left more in the world. It's the 'normal' social-based world construction that I find difficult to be in.

This Autistic spectrum is so much bigger than it looks from the outside. I experience so many things which the 'experts' can't define and don't quite have words for...yet. It's a realm of diversity caused by a mind and body wired in a profoundly different way. In ways that dictate my behaviour and leave me suffering at the hands of others not prepared to understand - other people unprepared to get to know who I am on the inside and who hurt me. Really.

Hullo. Mum, Dad, what are you doing to stop Autism and Asperger's from remaining one of the least recognised, least diagnosed, least accommodated and least supported disabilities of the modern era? Despite these things, it is also one of the largest and most disabling conditions... worldwide. Mum, Dad, could you help the world to know this, please? I want a world to be a part of. I want my community. I want my culture. I want them to thrive. I want acceptance for myself and those of my kind.

If I am like a goldfish on the telephone table, flapping and gasping, do not treat my gasps as tardive dyskinesia - with medication. Do not anaesthetize my tail, eh... put me back in my goldfish bowl - I was never meant to be a fish out of water!

I am here the way I am here because God 'saw the need'. Now what's that, eh? Let's find out together. This is gonna be fun.

Don't grieve for me anymore. Or for yourself and all you're gonna miss out on because of how I am. If ya gotta grieve, cry for a world that doesn't understand me. Grieve for everything other people will miss out on by not getting to know me. Better still, join me in this adventure free of grief...it will be fun.

I have decided for you,
and that is all my love,
(till I meet my other half perhaps,
by such time my heart will have grown,
and there never need be any loss felt by all,
...on the contrary),

Your son,
Johnny

APPENDIX

Helpful Books and Resources for Parents

Attwood, T. (1998). *Asperger's Syndrome: A Guide for Parents and Professionals.*
    London: Jessica Kingsley.

Barnhill, G. (2002). *Right Address…Wrong Planet: Children with Asperger Syndrome Becoming Adults.*
    Shawnee Mission, Kansas: Autism Asperger Publishing Co.

Bolick, T. (2001). *Asperger Syndrome and Adolescence: Helping Preteens and Teens Get Ready
    for the Real World.* Gloucester, MA: Fair Winds Press.

Grandin, T. (1996). *Thinking In Pictures: And Other Reports from My Life with Autism.*
    New York, NY: Vintage Books.

Heinrichs, R. (2003). *Perfect Targets: Asperger Syndrome and Bullying.* Shawnee Mission, Kansas:
    Autism Asperger Publishing Co.

Hutten, M. *The Asperger's Comprehensive Handbook: Help for Parents of Asperger's Children and Teens*
    (Available for edownload on www.myaspergerschild.com).

Jackson, L. (2002). *Freaks, geeks and asperger syndrome: A user guide to adolescence.*
    London England: Jessica Kingsley Publishers.

Newport, J., Newport M. (2002). *Autism-Asperger's & Sexuality: Puberty and Beyond.*
    Arlington, TX: Future Horizons.

Prince-Hughes, D. (2002). *Aquamarine Blue 5: Personal Stories of College Students with Autism.*
    Chicago, IL: Swallow Press.

Robison, J. (2007). *Look Me in the Eye: My Life with Asperger's.* New York: Crown.

Willey, L. H. (2001). *Asperger Syndrome in the Family: Redefining Normal.* London: Jessica Kingsley.

Bibliography

Adolescent Mood Swings. *ScienceDaily.* Retrieved January 26, 2012, from http://www.sciencedaily.com /releases/2007/03/070311202019.htm.

American Psychiatric Association. 2000. *Diagnostic and Statistical Manual of Mental Disorders,* 4th ed., text revision. Washington, DC, American Psychiatric Association.

Attwood T. 1998. *Asperger's Syndrome: A Guide for Parents and Professionals.* London: Jessica Kingsley Publishers.

Attwood, Tony. 2006. "Asperger's syndrome and problems related to stress." In *Stress and coping in autism,* 351-370. New York, NY US: Oxford University Press.

Attwood, T. 2007. The Complete Guide to Asperger's Syndrome. London: Jessica Kingsley Publishers.

Attwood S, Powell J. 2008. *Making Sense Of Sex: A Forthright Guide To Puberty, Sex And Relationships For People With Asperger's Syndrome* [e-book]. London England: Jessica Kingsley Publishers.

Badenoch, B. & Bogdan, 2012. *Safety and Connection: The Neurobiology of Play.* In *Play-Based Interventions for Children and Adolescents with Autism Spectrum Disorders* (Gallo-Lopez, L. & Rubin, L. C. Editors) New York, NY: Routledge.

Baron-Cohen, S. 1995. *Mindblindness: An essay on autism and theory of mind.* Cambridge, MA: The MIT Press.

Bromfield, R. 2010. *Doing Therapy with Children and Adolescents with Asperger Syndrome.* Hoboken, NJ: John Wiley & Sons Inc.

Fitzgerald, M. and Bellgrove, M. A. (2006). "The Overlap between Alexithymia and Asperger's Syndrome." *Journal of Autism and Developmental Disorders,* 36(4), 573–576. doi:10.1007/ s10803–006–0096-z.

Gellar, L. 2005. "Emotional Regulation and Autism Spectrum Disorders." *Autism Spectrum Quarterly.* (Summer, 2005). Retrieved from www.aspfi.org/documents/gellerasq.pdf.

Gillberg, C. 1991."Clinical and Neurobiological Aspects of Asperger's Syndrome in Six Families Studied." In *Autism and Asperger's Syndrome* (ed. U. Frith), 122–46. Cambridge: Cambridge University Press.

Hénault, Isabelle. 2006. *Asperger's syndrome and sexuality: From adolescence through adulthood.* London England: Jessica Kingsley Publishers.

Hull, Kevin. 2011. *Play Therapy and Asperger's Syndrome: Helping Children and Adolescents Grow, Connect, and Heal through the Art of Play.* Lanham, MD: Jason Aronson.

Jackson, Luke. 2002. *Freaks, Geeks and Asperger Syndrome: A User Guide to Adolescence.* London England: Jessica Kingsley Publishers.

Rao, P. A., Beidel, D. C., and Murray, M. J. 2008. "Social Skills Interventions for Children with Asperger's Syndrome or High-Functioning Autism: A Review and Recommendations." *Journal of Autism and Developmental Disorders,* 38(2), 353–61. doi:10.1007/s10803–007–0402–4.

Schultz, D. Franklin. 2005. *A Language Of The Heart, Therapy Stories That Heal.* Florida: Rainbow Books.

Sisk, Cheryl L, and Julia L Zehr. 2005. "Pubertal hormones organize the adolescent brain and behavior." *Frontiers In Neuroendocrinology* 26, no. 3-4: 163-174.

Willey, Lianne Holliday. 2003. *Asperger Syndrome in Adolescence: Living with the Ups, the Downs, and Things in Between.* London England: Jessica Kingsley Publishers.

INDEX

About the Author

Kevin B. Hull, Ph.D, LMHC, owns a private counseling practice in Lakeland, Florida where he has practiced for the past twelve years. Kevin specializes in using play therapy with children and adolescents diagnosed with Asperger's syndrome and high functioning autism and leads groups for young people in addition to helping to build connection between parents and young people on the autism spectrum. Prior to working in private practice, he worked in numerous community mental health settings. He was an adjunct professor for Webster University's Masters of Counseling Lakeland Campus for eight years and currently serves as an adjunct professor for Liberty University Online Masters of Counseling program. He and his wife Wendy have four children, a Dachshund, Quaker parrot, Guinea pig, and many fish.

CPSIA information can be obtained
at www.ICGtesting.com
Printed in the USA
BVHW050653031221
622944BV00003B/48

9 781935 986447